AN INTRODUCTION TO BIBLICAL ARCHAEOLOGY

Studies in Theology

Groundwork of The Philosophy of Religion By Atkinson Lee
The Poetry of the Old Testament By Theodore H. Robinson
Prophecy and the Prophets in Ancient Israel By Theodore H. Robinson
A Short Comparative History of Religions By Theodore H. Robinson
Religious Ideas of the Old Testament By H. Wheeler Robinson
The History of Israel By H. Wheeler Robinson
The Doctrine of the Atonement By J. K. Mozley
An Introduction to the Study of Some Living Religions of the East By Sydney Cave
Christianity and Some Living Religions of the East By Sydney Cave
The Christian Estimate of Man By Sydney Cave
The Doctrine of the Person of Christ By Sydney Cave
The Theology of the Epistles By H. A. A. Kennedy
Form Criticism By E. Basil Redlich
Faith and its Psychology By W. R. Inge
Christianity According to St. John By W. F. Howard
Christianity: Its Nature and Truth By A. S. Peake
Calvinism By A. Dakin
The Doctrine of the Trinity By Robert S. Franks
The Text of the Greek Bible By Sir Frederic Kenyon
The Text and Canon of the New Testament By Alexander Souter and C. S. C. Williams
The Apostolic Age By G. B. Caird
The Interpretation of the Bible By James D. Wood
A Critical Introduction to the Old Testament By G. W. Anderson

AN INTRODUCTION TO BIBLICAL ARCHAEOLOGY

by

G. ERNEST WRIGHT

assisted by

ROGER TOMES

GERALD DUCKWORTH & CO. LTD.

3 HENRIETTA STREET, LONDON, W.C.2

First published in 1960

Printed in Great Britain by Richard Clay and Company, Ltd.,
Bungay, Suffolk

FOREWORD

SOME years ago Dr. Nathaniel Micklem, editor of Duckworth's *Studies in Theology*, asked me to prepare a volume on biblical archaeology for the series. I began the revision and rewriting of an unpublished manuscript, started before the War and unfinished. When the work was but half completed it became apparent that the volume would be much too large for the purpose. The result was *Biblical Archaeology*, a lavishly illustrated volume that appeared in 1957, and was soon translated into German and Dutch.

The present volume is a condensation of the larger book by the Rev. Roger Tomes of Gomersal, Leeds. I am greatly indebted to him for his sympathetic and intelligent work. There has been some slight rearrangement of material, some touching up here and there to meet the exigencies of a rapidly developing field of study, and a great deal of omission, though the main points are all here. It is my hope that readers of the book may gain from it a fresh appreciation of the vast effort that has been and is being made to understand the Bible and biblical faith over against its setting in the ancient world.

G. ERNEST WRIGHT

Harvard Divinity School
August, 1959

CONTENTS

	FOREWORD	v
	INTRODUCTION	ix
	ABBREVIATIONS	xii
I.	THE RELIGION OF ISRAEL AND THE RELIGION OF CANAAN	1
II.	THE PATRIARCHS	21
III.	EXODUS AND CONQUEST	34
IV.	THE PERIOD OF THE JUDGES	53
V.	THE GOLDEN AGE	66
VI.	DIVISION AND DOWNFALL	90
VII.	THE LAST DAYS OF JUDAH	108
VIII.	AFTER THE EXILE	128
IX.	PALESTINE IN THE TIME OF CHRIST	147
X.	THE CHURCH IN THE WORLD	164
	INDEX	189

INTRODUCTION

THE Bible, unlike other religious literature of the world, is not centered in a series of moral, spiritual, and liturgical teachings, but in the story of a people who lived at a certain time and place. Biblical man learned to confess his faith by telling the story of what had happened to his people and by seeing within it the hand of God. Biblical faith is the knowledge of life's meaning in the light of what God did in a particular history. Thus the Bible cannot be understood unless the history it relates is taken seriously. Knowledge of biblical history is essential to the understanding of biblical faith.

In reconstructing the history of biblical times one comes upon many periods which are not well known from the surviving written records. If the nature of such periods is to be properly understood, and the biblical events fitted into their context in ancient history as a whole, the original background to the biblical material must be recovered with the aid of archaeology. As a result of the archaeological investigations of the last one hundred years, it is now possible to tell in great detail the story of the civilization of the ancient Near East, of which the story of Israel is a part. The biblical archaeologist, therefore, studies the results of the excavations in order to glean from them every fact that throws a direct, indirect, or even diffused light upon the Bible.

The study of archaeology, however, involves the theologian in certain risks. The first is that he may find that the biblical events did not occur at all, that the Bible is little more than a congeries of myth and legend. For the most part archaeology has substantiated and illumined the biblical story at so many crucial points that no one can seriously take this position. Nevertheless, the role of archaeology has sometimes been negative. For example, it has lent its support to the evidence of geology and biology that man and the earth have a much longer past than the traditional biblical chronology allowed. It has to be admitted that there are numerous historical problems which archaeology cannot solve because there is not enough evidence. In addition, there is in the Bible an interpretation of events and of experience which is not subject to historical or archaeological testing. That a violent wave of destruction occurred in southern Palestine in the 13th century B.C. is clear from the excavations. That this was caused by the Israelite invasion is a reasonable historical inference. That the warfare was directed by God for his own righteous ends is, however, an interpretation by faith which is not subject to historical testing. The resurrection of Christ was an inner certainty to early Christians, but it is something which archaeology can do nothing to illuminate. Hence the support archaeology can give to the biblical record is limited. It cannot 'prove the Bible true', but it can illuminate the historical setting, the events themselves, and the cultural background. The vast majority of the finds neither prove nor disprove: they fill in the background and give the setting for the story.

The second risk involved in studying the history of the Chosen People as we would that of any other people is that the parallels to biblical history and culture thrown up by the discoveries may destroy their uniqueness. It may be stated emphatically, however, that to those who have been willing to take this risk the literature of Israel and of the Church appears more distinctive than ever before. We can see that though the Bible arose in the ancient world, it was not entirely of it; though its history and its people resemble those of the surrounding nations, yet it radiates an atmosphere, a spirit, a faith far more profound than, and radically different from, that of any other ancient literature. In the opening chapter we shall compare the faith of Israel and the polytheism of her neighbours, and show how archaeology has emphasized the distinctiveness of biblical faith.

ABBREVIATIONS

ANE	J. B. Pritchard (ed.), *The Ancient Near East: An Anthology of Texts and Pictures* (Princeton, 1959)
ANEP	J. B. Pritchard (ed.), *The Ancient Near East in Pictures relating to the Old Testament* (Princeton, 1954)
ANET	J. B. Pritchard (ed.), *Ancient Near Eastern Texts relating to the Old Testament* (Princeton, 1950; 2nd ed., 1955)
BA	*The Biblical Archaeologist*
BASOR	*Bulletin of the American Schools of Oriental Research*
BJRL	*Bulletin of the John Rylands Library*
DOTT	D. Winton Thomas (ed.), *Documents from Old Testament Times* (Edinburgh, 1958)
ECW	F. van der Meer and C. Mohrmann, *Atlas of the Early Christian World* (tr. and ed. by M. F. Hedlund and H. H. Rowley) (Edinburgh, 1958)
Grollenberg	L. H. Grollenberg, *Atlas of the Bible* (tr. and ed. by J. M. H. Reid and H. H. Rowley) (Edinburgh, 1957)
JBL	*Journal of Biblical Literature*
RHR	*Revue d'Histoire des Religions*
WHA	G. E. Wright and F. V. Filson, *The Westminster Historical Atlas to the Bible* (Philadelphia, 1945; 5th ed., 1958)
Wiseman	D. J. Wiseman, *Illustrations from Biblical Archaeology* (London, 1958)
Wright	G. E. Wright, *Biblical Archaeology* (Philadelphia and London, 1957)

CHAPTER I

THE RELIGION OF ISRAEL AND THE RELIGION OF CANAAN

In this chapter we shall discuss Israel's faith in relation to the religions of her environment. Only within recent years has the progress of archaeological study reached the point where we can begin to speak with confidence about the theology of the ancient polytheisms around Israel. This means that it is now possible to make certain emphases in describing biblical faith which formerly were not entirely clear; we can do so because we have more knowledge of the relation and reaction of the faith to its environment.

God and the Gods

In polytheism the gods were actually the elements and powers in the world, personalized and given names. The primary setting of divine life was thus nature, and the life of nature was the life of the gods.

Since there was nothing outside the world to create it, thought about the origin of the world could not reach behind the primordial static chaos, which was conceived as the primeval ocean or 'deeps' from which the salt and fresh waters on earth come. In Mesopotamia the 'deeps' were personified as a male and female pair, Apsu and Tiamat, and creation began by sexual procreation on their part. They produced a series of gods, the various elements of the universe as then understood. Order was achieved after a cosmic battle among the gods in which the younger active forces, headed by their king, defeated the static chaos. Apsu was killed by magic; Tiamat was cut in two, one half becoming heaven and the other earth; and the gods were divided, one half in heaven and the other on earth, charged with their respective duties. Man was created as the slave of the gods to do the menial work of the earth. A human king was chosen by the divine council and charged with the social order on earth. Society was a human contrivance, not an order of creation or of revelation. Life was uncertain, and the creation-battle had to be refought each year in a New Year's ritual drama in which the king took the role of the king of the gods.

In Egypt the same once-for-all and yet yearly (and also daily) battle was waged by Re (the Sun) against the dragon of chaos and darkness. Yet in Egypt life was not as precarious as in Mesopotamia. Victory was always assured; society and world-order were static and rhythmic, fixed in the order of creation. Hence other approaches to the creation were made which emphasized the fullness and glory of the present order, such as the emergence from the ocean of chaos of the hill on which Re, the primeval king, began the creation by an act of masturbation. The security of the social order on earth was assured because the king was not a human being but a divine incarnation, the son of Re.

In Canaan the creation doctrine was evidently similar to that of Babylon in its main essentials, though we do not know so much about it. Creation was described as a battle between Baal, the king of the gods, and the primordial dragon of chaos, called Leviathan (Lotan) or Sea (Yam). The Old Testament has a number of allusions to this symbol of chaos, using the terms 'serpent', 'dragon' or 'monster', and 'Rahab', as well as 'Leviathan' and 'Sea' (e.g.,

Ps. 74. 13–14; 89. 10; Job 3. 8, where 'day' should be rendered 'Sea'; Job 41; Isa. 27. 1; 51. 9; Amos 9. 3). This is also the source of the 'beast' in Revelation, the account of whose destruction ends with the significant words, 'the sea was no more' (Rev. 21. 1).

The polytheist thought of creation, then, in terms of a struggle between the various powers of nature, and of world order as an achievement in harmony among many wills. It was believed that some principle of order had been established at creation, to which even the gods were subject. Mankind has its fate, a destination given it before existence. Biblical faith, on the other hand, did not believe in any *principle* of world order as such, nor in a fixed impersonal destiny for mankind. This world order is not fixed and eternal; God is engaged in a struggle with an estranged world, so that what we now see is not final.

One of the most important things about nature is its orderly movement in the cycle of night and day and in the regular return of the seasons. In the polytheisms life and history were believed to move with the powers of nature in their never-ending cycle. This meant that the basic religious literature of the polytheist was not primarily concerned with history or with the life of man on earth, but with the life of the gods, which is the life of nature. The myths, the stories of the loves and wars of the gods, as told, for example, in the Babylonian creation epic, explained to a particular society the way of the universe to which it must adjust.

It is misleading to apply the same term 'myth' to certain characteristics of the Bible, such as its view of the world as a small space protected by the heavens in the midst of the great 'deeps', its interpretation of history in terms of God's activity, and many of its stories such as those of Adam and

Eve, the divine covenant, the miracles, the incarnation and resurrection of Jesus. Nothing could be more different than the Bible as a whole from polytheist mythology. The Bible is first of all a historical literature, not removed and separate from human life. Life and history are not cyclical, dependent on nature's rhythm, but move in a direction that God wills.

The God the Bible proclaims is the Lord of history. He is not nature personified or any element in nature. He is the independent and self-existing source or Creator of nature and all that is. As Creator he is distinct from what he has made, and as Ruler he is not what he rules. For this reason Israel could not view the creation as a struggle, but as an act of the one Deity. Genesis 1 therefore begins with God, who exists before the creation. Yet Hebrew thought started like polytheism with the watery deep and primeval darkness. *Tehom*, the word for the 'deep', is from the same original word as the Babylonian Tiamat. But the 'deep' is not a dragon or a person. While making the world God also created the world's time, day and night, the week, and the seasons. Hence the creation does not suggest to the Hebrew a timeless, cosmic pattern, but instead the beginning of time and history.

We must suppose that Israel came to its understanding of God in a different way from the polytheist, through some outstanding event in history. This according to the biblical record was the Exodus from Egypt. A great Power, greater than Pharaoh or anything in the world, delivered the people from Egyptian slavery. In so doing he showed his complete control over the forces of nature, and revealed at least in outline his intentions and purposes. Thus Israel was intensely interested in history, and became the first people on earth to preserve a connected account of its own history, because the events of this earth are revelations of God, and to tell them is to confess one's faith. The primary views which the Bible has about God have been inferred from historical events. This was what caused Israel to de-myth the creation myths of antiquity, and to infer that God was the sole Creator because he is Lord of all.

Israel's understanding of man was likewise very different from that of polytheism. Man possessed dignity and worth because he was given the freedom to be a responsible being. The dignity of man is given to him by God; man does not possess a divine 'spark', nor the ability to become God or even to unite or fuse with God in some mystical exercise. God has preserved his independence from what he has created.

It is doubtful whether Israel rejected entirely the polytheist view of nature as alive and full of power. In Gen. 1 the heavenly bodies are not gods as they were in polytheism; they are simply God's lights as fixed in heaven's firmament. Yet the words in v. 26 ('Let us make man') and those in Gen. 3. 22 (Man the sinner 'has become like one of us') indicate that God has other supernatural beings associated with him. Jacob's dream (Gen. 28. 10–17) depicts a view of God's rule over the earth through his angels or heavenly messengers. In Isa. 6 and in many similar passages in prophecy God is represented as sitting on his heavenly throne with his angelic ministers surrounding him. The phrase 'sons of God', which was the usual term for the gods of Canaan in Canaanite polytheism, for they were believed to be literally the children of the great gods and goddesses, was taken over in Israelite circles as a designation for God's heavenly host. We are not left in doubt that the host of heaven included the sun, moon, planets, and stars. The leaders of the faith struggled against the worship of anything in heaven or earth, except God alone (e.g., Deut. 4. 19). Yet the heavenly bodies continued to be identified as members of God's heavenly court, even in pious circles (e.g., Neh. 9. 6; Ps. 148) which did not give them worship. The Israelites did not break so radically with polytheist conceptions that they began to think of an inanimate nature.

It is now necessary to turn our attention from polytheism in general to the one religion which gave Israel more trouble than any other. This is the religion of Canaan, of Israel's immediate neighbors. Until recent years our knowledge of Canaanite religion was largely confined to the pages of the Old Testament and to excerpts from Phoenician writings quoted chiefly by later writers. Now, however, a portion of their long lost religious literature has been recovered, from the library discovered by a French expedition at Ras Shamra (the ancient Ugarit) in northern Syria in 1929.

The Gods of Canaan

The general Canaanite word for 'god' or 'divinity' was *el*, and 'gods' were called either by the plural of this word or by the phrase 'sons of god', which really means, in Semitic idiom, 'members of the divine family'. The chief of all the gods, or the head of the divine family, was called 'El'. He is a rather shadowy figure who apparently takes little part in the affairs of men. He lives far away 'at the source of the (two) rivers, in the midst of the fountains of the two deeps', i.e., in the underworld, which was thought to be the source both of the fresh-water springs and rivers and of the salt-water oceans.

El's wife seems to have been Asherah. While she was

originally the mother-goddess, in practice her functions are frequently mixed with those of the goddesses of fertility. In the Old Testament we have a number of allusions to Asherah, though her name is hidden in the Authorized Version by the translation 'grove'. Jezebel introduced into Israel four hundred prophets of Asherah (1 Kings 18. 19), and Manasseh had an image of her put in the Temple (2 Kings 21. 7). The symbol of her presence at a place of worship was apparently a sacred tree or pole standing near the altar (1 Kings 16. 33; 2 Kings 21. 3). Such objects must have been very familiar, for we constantly hear the injunction that they should be cut down, burned, or pulled up because they led Israel astray (Deut. 7. 5; 12. 3; 16. 21; Mic. 5. 14; etc.).

Chief among the offspring of El and Asherah, either as son or grandson, was Baal, the most colorful and important of all the gods. Baal was originally the god's title and not his proper name. The latter was Hadad, though by the 15th/14th centuries B.C. the title was in use almost exclusively. The Canaanite word *baal* simply meant 'lord', and could be applied to any one of a number of gods, but the Lord or Baal above all others was thought to be the great god who controlled the rain and therefore the vegetation. His home was on a mountain in the far-away north, at the edge of the world where earth and heaven meet. This is probably to be identified with Tyre's 'Holy Mountain' (Ezek. 28. 14) and 'Mount Zion in the recesses of the North (Saphon)' (Ps. 48. 2).

Baal is called 'Zabul (the Exalted), Lord of earth', a title which is preserved also in the Old Testament in the mention of the god Baal-zebul (not Baal-zebub) at Ekron (2 Kings 1. 2). By New Testament times Baal-zebul had become a title for Satan (e.g., Mt. 12. 24). Baal is also called 'Lord of heaven' and 'the Rider of the Clouds', a title actually given to God (see Ps. 68. 4 RSV).

It is interesting to note that in Israel God took over some of the titles and functions of these Canaanite gods, particularly those of Baal. *El* and *Baal* are both used as names for Yahweh, the God of Israel. The existence of such names as Ishbaal ('man of Baal' or 'Baal exists'), Beeliada ('may Baal know') and Bealiah ('Yahweh is Baal') does not mean that the Canaanite Baal was worshipped, but that the title was given Yahweh. Yet the danger of confusion and syncretism was so great that in the course of time *baal* was dropped. See, e.g., Hos. 2. 17: 'And I shall remove the *baal* names from her (Israel's) mouth, and they shall no longer be remembered in their (Israel's) name(s).' Another Canaanite term for 'lord', *Adon*, continued in common use as a divine title. *Elyon*, meaning 'exalted' or 'most high', was still another Canaanite title frequently used for Yahweh of Israel.

Baal as the active suzerain of the universe would obviously have been active in many spheres which Yahweh claimed for his own. Particularly is this true with regard to the storm which Baal personified. Lightning became Yahweh's arrow and thunder his voice (Ps. 18. 13–14). God's dramatic appearances on earth could be depicted as a storm, with dark cloud or smoke, thunder or trumpet blast, lightning and the shaking of the earth which accompanies great thunder (Ex. 19. 16 ff.; 1 Kings 19. 11–12). Psalm 29, dominated by this type of nature imagery, is now believed to have been originally a hymn to Baal, borrowed and used of Yahweh. It is Yahweh, not Baal, who 'maketh the hinds to calve' (Ps. 29. 9), and gives the blessings of heaven (rain), of the deep (springs and rivers), of breast and womb (Gen. 49. 25; Deut. 33. 13 ff.).

Baal's wife was Anath, a goddess of love and war, whom the Egyptians depicted as a naked woman on a galloping horse, brandishing shield and lance. One of her bloody escapades is depicted in a Ras Shamra poem. Yet, in spite of her warlike and sadistic nature, she was the goddess of love and fertility. In these functions she was similar to the goddess Astarte, or Ashtoreth, as her name is spelt in the Old Testament. These goddesses were responsible for the productivity of animals and man. In an Egyptian text they are called 'the great goddesses who conceive but do not bear'. In the Old Testament we hear almost nothing of Anath, but a great deal of Ashtoreth (1 Sam. 31. 10; 1 Kings 11. 5; 2 Kings 23. 13; etc.). It is probable that among the Canaanites there was never agreement as to which of these goddesses was the wife of Baal. At Ras Shamra it was Anath; in the Old Testament Ashtoreth is customarily associated with Baal (Jdg. 2. 13; 10. 6; 1 Sam. 7. 4; 12. 10); Jezebel of Tyre associated Asherah with Baal in her worship (1 Kings 18. 19).

The major gods and goddesses of Canaan were apparently pictured as having human form, though there were many minor beings who were conceived as birds or animals or hybrids. At least so we might judge from contemporary art. The amazing thing about the gods, however, is that there seems to have been no standard of morality governing their actions. Goodness and godliness did not go together. The lives of the gods were certainly on a moral level below that of the average of society, if we can judge from the ancient codes of law.

The primary purpose of the stories about the gods was to explain the world and how it works. We shall mention here only that myth which received most attention in Canaan, the essentials of which were present and popular throughout the Near East. To understand it we must know something about the climate of Palestine. From April to the end of October there is no rain, except for a very occasional unseasonable shower. Only those vegetables and plants can grow which can secure what water they need from the heavy morning dew. Toward the end of October the rains begin, and continue, on and off, throughout the winter to the end of April. The winter, therefore, is one general rainy season, though the Israelites generally divided it into two parts: the early rains (*yoreh*) and the spring rains (*malqosh*). Very early in the spring, about February, the grain is planted, while harvest is in May or June, though the exact time varies with the season and the part of the country. In April, as a result of the rains, the whole countryside is covered with verdure, including beautiful wild flowers of all sorts. By the end of May these have all disappeared, and the landscape is barren except for the trees and the occasional thorny bush which can survive the dry season.

The Canaanite, personifying the forces of nature, explained the cycle thus. Rain-and-Vegetation (the god Baal) was killed each spring after a great battle with Death (Mot) or with the 'Devourers' and 'Renderers', who at Ras Shamra were a group of beings fulfilling the same function. Thus through the summer months Death and the destructive forces reigned supreme. Why do the rains begin again in the fall? Because Death is vanquished by Baal's warrior wife, and Baal comes back to life. Why does verdure cover the land in the spring? Because of the mating of Baal and Fertility, his wife (either Anath or Ashtoreth).

Periods of drought and famine were probably explained in the same way. The Ras Shamra story in which Baal was apparently killed by the 'Devourers' and 'Renderers' may not refer to the yearly cycle at all, but to a drought. We are told that after his death 'El completed seven years, eight yearly cycles, while he (Baal) was clad with the blood of his brethren as a garment, with the blood of his companions as a cloak'. During that time 'the king ceased to give judgment, women ceased to draw water from the spring, the well of the temple ceased to yield water and the sound of work ceased in the workshop'. After Death was destroyed, one of the gods had a dream in which he saw that

> The heavens rained oil;
> the valleys ran honey;
> So I know that triumphant Baal lives,
> that the prince, lord of earth, exists.

This myth of the dying–rising god was common throughout the Near East. In Babylonia he was called Tammuz, and his wife (Love and Fertility) was Ishtar. In Egypt it was Osiris and Isis, and in Greece Adonis and Aphrodite. While the stories in these countries, as in Canaan, were greatly elaborated in numerous ways, the basic plot is as outlined above.

There can be no doubt that the Israelites were well acquainted with this myth, for we find hints of it in several places. It seems probable, for example, that the prophet Hosea makes use of words, phrases, and imagery drawn from the Canaanite worship of Baal (Hos. 6. 1–3; N.B. 'He will bring us to life (again) after two days; On the third day he will raise us up' and 'He will come to us like the rain, Like the spring rain he will water the earth').

It is possible also that the frequent emphasis in the Old Testament on Yahweh as the 'living God' may have been an Israelite reaction to the belief in the dying–rising Baal (cf. Hab. 1. 12 RV margin: 'Art not thou from everlasting, O Lord my God, mine Holy One? thou diest not').

WORSHIP

While we know a good deal about the mythology of the ancient Near East, we do not know as much as we would like about the religious practices and attitudes of the common man. We have noted already his belief that nature was alive and full of strange forces. It was imperative that he develop ways and means of controlling these forces. His religion accordingly was centered round a variety of acts, designed to turn the attention of the gods to him that they might prosper his ways. There was little in his religion that might make him a better man. Society had its laws, and these were given religious sanction, but the primary attention was toward those ritual acts which would make the gods more favorable to him.

The religion of Canaan, as we know it from Ras Shamra and from the Old Testament, undoubtedly involved elaborate systems of ritual, especially sacrificial ritual. A large variety of animals and birds are known to have been used. From numerous biblical and Roman allusions we know also that child sacrifice was occasionally practised, the story of the Moabite king Mesha (2 Kings 3. 27) immediately coming to mind. Many jars with children's bones have been found in the excavations, but infant mortality was exceedingly high, and we can be sure that most cases of child burial which have been found do not indicate child-sacrifice. From numerous allusions also we know that various forms of divination, ways of peering into the future, were common among the Canaanites (see, e.g., Deut. 18. 10).

The chief emphasis in Canaanite religion, however, was upon fertility and sex. Worship therefore would be concerned first of all with the problem of making land, herds, flocks, and human beings fertile and productive. It is probable that many of the mythological stories were acted out in the religious festivals, especially at the spring festival, when the mating of Rain-and-Vegetation (Baal) with the goddess of Fertility was supposed to have taken place. In any event, we know that sacred prostitution, both male and female, was exceedingly common, practised in the name of religion at the various centers of worship. The fertility goddess was actually represented by a sacred prostitute, called 'the Holy One'. In Egypt she was pictured as a nude woman, standing on a lion, with a lily or lilies (symbolizing her charm or sex appeal) in one hand and a serpent or two (symbolizing fecundity) in the other. Similar representations on clay plaques, which must also represent the fertility goddess in her role of 'the Holy One', have been found in large numbers in the towns of late Canaanite Palestine. There were probably one or more of these in every home. Perhaps it was thought that by handling such sacred and magical objects, fertility would be imparted to the one in need.

The sexual emphasis of Canaanite religion was certainly extreme, and at its worst could have appealed only to the baser side of man. Such religion appeared sordid and degrading to religious circles in Israel. There is a direct prohibition of sacred prostitution in Deut. 23. 17–18.

Most of the common worship was carried on at the 'high places', where there were sacrificial altars (cf. 1 Sam. 9. 12; 1 Kings 3. 4). The best example of a Canaanite altar for burnt offering has been found at Megiddo, dating from about 1900 B.C. At the foot of it were found quantities of animal bones, the remains of sacrifices which had been burned on the top of the altar.

According to the Old Testament, Canaanite high places had other sacred objects beside the altar. One was the sacred tree, grove or post, which the prophetic writings exhorted the people to cut down. We have already noticed that these objects were apparently the symbols of the mother-goddess Asherah. The sacred tree was very common in ancient Near Eastern religion, as we know not only from texts but also from ancient art. It even appears in the Garden of Eden (Gen. 2. 9). Also present at most Canaanite high places was the sacred pillar, quite a number of which have been found both in Palestine and Transjordan. Good arguments have been advanced to connect these pillars with ancestor-veneration, but it is difficult to explain all of them in this way. At the high places, if the sacred tree is the symbol of the mother-goddess, it is possible that the pillar may have been the symbol of El or Baal. In some late representations of Phoenician temples the pillar occupies the central place in the sanctuary, just where we should expect a statue of the deity.

From various excavations in Palestine have come small limestone altars with 'horns' on the corners, the earliest having been found at Megiddo in a shrine of the Israelite period, dating about the time of David or shortly thereafter (early 10th century). These altars are too small for burnt offerings and could only have been used for incense. Recently one such object was found in North Syria, belonging to a much later period, but having the word *hamman* inscribed upon it. The word *hammanim* occurs some eight times in the Old Testament (Lev. 26. 30; 2 Chr. 14. 5; 34. 4, 7; Isa. 17. 8; 27. 9; Ezek. 6. 4, 6). The meaning has in the past been obscure, but we are now justified in rendering 'altar of incense'. Enlightened religious circles in Israel and Judah considered such objects pagan and condemned them along with the pillars and trees or posts.

High places were only country sanctuaries, however; there were many more elaborate places of worship situated in Canaanite cities. It was commonly believed that the gods needed houses to live in, just as men did. One of the Ras Shamra myths tells about the erection of a temple for Baal, and this temple and many others have been excavated in Palestine and Syria. A series of them has been found at Beth-shan, dating from the 14th to the 10th century. A well-preserved Canaanite temple found at Lachish was destroyed about 1220 B.C. by the Hebrews, obviously while in full use as a sanctuary. In the debris large numbers of animal and bird bones were found, all the upper part of the right foreleg. This is exactly what we should expect from the biblical law concerning peace offerings, since the portion of the priests was the right shoulder (Lev. 7. 32 RV margin). Presumably the rest could be eaten by the worshippers outside or in some neighboring chamber. Few of the bones showed evidence of burning, indicating that the meat had been cooked by boiling (cf. 1 Sam. 2. 12 ff.).

Few large idols have been found in Palestine and Syria. Monumental stones with pictures of the gods upon them have been discovered, however, and also large numbers of small metal images, mainly of male deities, particularly Baal. There are several descriptions of these small metal figures in the Old Testament, e.g., Hab. 2. 19. None of these have been found in Israelite towns, however, and we shall return to the possible significance of this fact below.

Canaanites (and Semites in general) believed that under the earth was the nether world, called in the Old Testament

'Sheol', or simply 'the pit'. When a man died he descended to the underworld and lived there with the 'shades', those who had gone before him. It was a cheerless, dark place, to which a man must go regardless of the quality of his life. In other words, the ideas of heaven, resurrection, and rewards in the after-life are not to be found in the religion of Canaan, nor in the religion of Israel (until the last pre-Christian centuries), for the Israelites shared the common Semitic heritage in this regard. Consequently the burial customs of Canaan and Israel are identical. Graves were usually shared by the members of a family (cf. the patriarchal cave of Machpelah). Here the bodies were interred along with objects which had been used in life, and which it was believed would be needed in the underworld. Jewelry, weapons, and pottery are the things most commonly found. Dishes, cups, and jars had been the invariable burial gifts since the invention of pottery; in them food and drink were placed for the dead to use on their journey to Sheol.

Such in brief was the religion of Canaan. What was Israel's reaction to it?

Israel and the Religion of Canaan

In the discussion of Canaanite religion a sufficient number of biblical allusions has been given to show something of the influence of the Semitic world in general and of the Canaanite world in particular upon the life of Israel. The Hebrew views of the world order, the sky, the earth, and the underworld were those of the Semitic world. So also was the belief that the proper way to worship was first of all to sacrifice an animal and to bring to the sanctuary gifts from the first fruits of the field, the flock, and the herd. Many of the rules by which sacrifices must be made were common property, and it is now evident that much of the sacrificial ritual found in the book of Leviticus was borrowed from Canaan. From Canaanite documents, particularly from the Ras Shamra tablets, we learn that at least some of the offerings have the same names in Canaan as in Israel. We are also reminded of the statement of Amos (5. 25) that the elaboration at least of this sacrificial ritual did not go back to Mosaic times, in which contention he was undoubtedly correct.

Even a casual reading of the Old Testament will indicate also that while the enlightened religious leadership of Israel might believe one way, the mass of the people were more tolerant of the ways of the world, adopting many of the practices of their neighbors, until large numbers of them were virtually polytheists.

Having noted the similarities, the borrowing, and the syncretism, let us now note a few of the differences.

The first remarkable fact about the Israelite conception of God is that he was believed to stand entirely alone, with no other being on his level. He is represented throughout the Old Testament as a 'jealous' god; that is, he is concerned that the people do not fall back into polytheism, that they worship and follow none but himself. He has no wife and family. In fact, biblical Hebrew possessed no word for 'goddess'. Enlightened religious circles apparently did not believe in a female principle as necessary to explain the working of the world, though to be sure many tolerant Israelites compromised their heritage in worshipping the gods and goddesses of Canaan.

Equally surprising is the prohibition of images (Ex. 20. 4; 34. 17). This is a significant commandment, since there was nothing like it in the world about. Archaeology offers support for the antiquity of this commandment in Israel in that a figure of Yahweh has yet to be found in the debris of an Israelite town, in contrast to the series of figurines of male deities found in Canaanite cities.[1] At the same time, however, large numbers of figurines representing the mother-goddess are found in every excavation into Israelite houses. They are indisputable evidence of the widespread syncretism, verging on polytheism, among the common people. They probably owned them, however, not so much for theological as for magical reasons, using them as 'good luck' charms.

Reference has already been made to the fact that typical mythology is not characteristic of biblical literature. The Israelite vocabulary of names for God was not drawn from nature but exclusively from human society. God is lord, king, judge, shepherd, father, husband, and the like. Such terms were also used in polytheism for the gods, but they were superimposed upon more central images from nature, such as sky, storm, the heavenly bodies, fertility, etc. Nature in the Bible, as God's creation, contained no forms on which man could focus his primary religious attention. The biblical representation of deity in human form exclusively (anthropomorphism) is a witness to God's personal relation to history and to human society, for the only possible image of him is the mental image of a person with whom man can have personal relations.

The worship of such a God could make use of many forms used by polytheists, but their inner intent would be different. In polytheism the worshipper stood before his deity with gifts to win his favor and to make atonement for his sins. In Israel the worshipper did the same, but there is

[1] After this was written, one example appeared in ruins of the Period of the Judges at Hazor in Galilee. From what the Bible says about idolatry, more of them would be expected.

much less faith in the power of a rite, no matter how well performed, to reconcile oneself with God unless there was also a real repentance. The whole world of pagan magic was discarded, including spiritualism, astrology, and divination; and so also was the world of demons, who in polytheism caused so much of life's misery, though in the inter-testamental age part of this world was allowed to enter the newly conceived dominion of Satan.

Texts and Illustrations

Texts

(p. 1) The Babylonian Story of Creation: *ANE*, 31–9; *ANET*, 60–72; *DOTT*, 3–16

(p. 2) Egyptian Creation stories: *ANET*, 3–10, 11–12

(p. 6) Ras Shamra texts: *ANE*, 92–132; *ANET*, 129–55; *DOTT*, 118–33

Illustrations (The references are to Figures)

(p. 6) Ras Shamra texts: *ANE*, 68; *DOTT*, 7; Wiseman, 26

(p. 9) Anath: *ANEP*, 479

(p. 13) Representations of fertility goddess: *ANEP*, 470–4; Wright, 68

(p. 13) Altar at Megiddo: Wright, 24

(p. 14) Sacred Tree: *ANEP*, Index, s.v. 'tree'; Wiseman, 6

(p. 14) Sacred Pillar: Wiseman, 112; Wright, 25, 69

(p. 14) Altars of incense: *ANE*, 148; *ANEP*, 575; Grollenberg, 195; Wright, 70

(p. 15) Temples at Beth-shan: *ANEP*, 732, 736–8; Grollenberg, 197; Wright, 59

(p. 15) Temple at Lachish: *ANE*, 187; *ANEP*, 731; Grollenberg, 196; Wright, 48

(p. 15) Images of Baal: *ANE*, 136; *ANEP*, 490; Grollenberg, 168, 170; Wiseman, 113; Wright, 62; *WHA*, 21

(p. 18) Mother-goddess figurines: *ANE*, 128; *ANEP*, 467–9; Grollenberg, 162–6; Wright, 72

CHAPTER II

THE PATRIARCHS

ARCHAEOLOGY has shed considerable light on the stories of the patriarchs in Genesis, Abraham, Isaac, and Jacob. Not that any records of these men have ever been found outside the Bible, but the veil which previously hid their times has been lifted. As a result, we now know more about the type of people they were, where they came from, how they lived, what they believed, where and how they are to be fitted into the histories of the great nations of ancient times than did the later Israelites themselves.

This does not mean that the patriarchal stories can be treated as a straightforward history of pre-Mosaic times. They are sagas, which were passed on orally for centuries before they were written down, very different from the histories in the books of Samuel and Kings. They also serve a religious theme, for the events they describe seemed to later ages to hold the promise of Israel's future destiny within them. Sometimes the fortunes of the patriarch (e.g., in the stories about Jacob and Esau) seem to be not so much those of an individual as those of the personified tribe. Occasional historical details have been modernized: the mention of camels in Genesis (e.g., 24. 10) is an anachronism, as the camel had not yet been generally domesticated; the Philistines appear in southern Palestine (Gen. 21. 34; 26) some five or six hundred years before their time.

We shall probably never be able to prove that Abraham

really existed, that he did or said this or that, but what we can prove is that his life and times, as reflected in the stories about him, fit perfectly within the early 2nd millennium, but imperfectly within any later period. This is one of the most important contributions which archaeology has made to Old Testament study during the last four decades.

The Original Home of the Patriarchs

According to the biblical tradition, the patriarchs were Aramaeans (Deut. 26. 5; Gen. 25. 20; 28. 5; 31. 20, 24). Their original home, with which they kept close touch, was Aram-Naharaim ('Aram of the Two Rivers', Gen. 24. 10) or Paddan-Aram ('The field of Aram', Gen. 25. 20). This was the land between the Euphrates and the Tigris in their upper courses, between Carchemish on the west and Nineveh on the east. Its chief city was Haran (Gen. 11. 31; 28. 10). Although the present text of the Old Testament tells us that Abraham's father Terah migrated to Haran from Ur, a great Sumerian city near the Persian Gulf, there is little evidence of any south Mesopotamian influence upon the patriarchal traditions. Haran was the home with which the patriarchs were most closely connected.

This association with Haran has been strengthened by the discovery that the names of several of Abraham's ancestors (Gen. 11. 10 ff.) are the names of towns in the vicinity. The name of one of Abraham's brothers was Haran, the same as that of the city itself, except that the two words begin with different kinds of *h*. Another brother was called Nahor (Gen. 24. 10): a town of that name is well known from the texts of the 18th century B.C. discovered at Mari on the Upper Euphrates and from Assyrian documents. The name of their father, Terah, appears in the name of the town Til-Turakhi; that of their great-grandfather, Serug, in Sarugi; that of an earlier ancestor, Peleg, in Phaliga. It would seem that the names of Abraham's brothers and ancestors were patriarchal clan names which were either given by the clans to towns which they founded or borrowed by them from towns which they had seized.

This second possibility has been mentioned because there is some reason to believe that the patriarchal clans were involved in the 'barbarian' invasions which brought to a temporary halt the flourishing cultures of the Near East about 2000 B.C. These were invasions of Semitic nomads from the desert fringes of the Fertile Crescent. They settled chiefly in northern Syria and Mesopotamia, where they were called 'Westerners' by the Babylonians, a name preserved in the Old Testament as 'Amorites'. Babylon itself became an Amorite state, to be ruled about 1700 by the great Hammurabi, and Amorite cities appeared all over Paddan-Aram and the area of modern Syria (Mari, Haran, Nahor, Qatna, Ugarit). The term 'Amorite' probably covered several closely related groups, one of which may have been the early Aramaeans.

At least the Haran area was one of the centres of the new Semitic settlements precisely at the time when the patriarchs are supposed to have been there. In addition, the names Abram (in the form *Abamram*) and Jacob (in the form *Jacob-el*) are known as personal names among the Amorites. There is frequent mention in the Mari library of a tribe of Benjaminites which was causing some trouble in the area, though of course there can be no direct connection with the later Israelite tribe of that name.

Another troublesome group at Mari was the *Hapiru*. People called by this name figure in early documents in various ways: as raiders, mercenary soldiers, captives, government employees, rebels, and slaves. In times of peace they worked in various capacities for the settled people. In unsettled periods they might raid the urban areas or hire themselves out as soldiers to the highest bidder. It is probable that the term does not apply to any particular nationality, religion, or language, but rather to a social or legal status. It seems likely that it was used for the unsettled nomadic people, among others, who haunted the civilized communities around the Arabian desert.

In the past *Hapiru* (or *'Apiru*, as it would have been pronounced in Canaanite) was identified with 'Hebrew', and although recent evidence has complicated the problem, we are fairly safe in assuming at least an indirect connection. Abraham is called 'the Hebrew' (Gen. 14. 13), and most references to 'Hebrews' in the Old Testament belong to the patriarchal period and that of the sojourn in Egypt. The usage of the term further suggests that, like *Hapiru*, 'Hebrew' did not refer originally to a particular racial group, but rather to the status of a foreigner.

Thus several lines of evidence meet to suggest that the patriarchs came from the nomadic invading peoples. Their own move south into Palestine would be part of this same movement.

Even more striking evidence for the north Mesopotamian origin of the patriarchs is provided by the archives of the city of Nuzi, a town south-east of Nineveh, which reveal a customary law similar to that of the patriarchs, but not like that of any later period. The Nuzians were Hurrians (the biblical 'Horites'), a non-Indo-European, Armenoid people who pushed into northern Mesopotamia and founded a great state in the 'Amorite' area during the 16th and 15th centuries, taking over much of the older 'Amorite' culture, including in all probability the customs in question.

Some of the Nuzi tablets explain how it was that someone outside the family could be Abraham's heir (Gen. 15. 2 ff.). It was the custom for a childless couple to adopt a son, who would take care of them as long as they lived and see to it that they received an honorable burial. In return for this service he inherited the property. The bargain was nullified, however, at least in part, if a son was born.

Esau's sale of his birthright to Jacob (Gen. 25. 30–34) is paralleled in the Nuzi tablets, where one brother sells a grove which he has inherited for three sheep! Isaac's inability to revoke the blessing which Jacob had extorted under false pretences (Gen. 27. 33) is illustrated by a case at Nuzi when such an oral 'blessing' was upheld in court.

Perhaps most interesting of all is the explanation of the relations between Jacob and Laban. Jacob was adopted by Laban as his heir, but his position was later threatened when sons were born to Laban (Gen. 30. 35). He therefore decided to return to Canaan with the fortune he had accumulated (Gen. 30. 31–31. 12), taking also the family gods or *teraphim*. Apparently, according to Nuzi law, possession of these idols not only helped to secure a successful life but also conferred the title to the family inheritance. Small wonder that Laban was far more excited about the loss of his *teraphim* than he was about the loss of his daughters, their husbands, and livestock.

It is also possible that the Old Testament traditions of human origins provide evidence for the Mesopotamian origin of the patriarchs. The stories of the Creation and the Flood in Gen. 2 and 6–9 do not resemble anything in Egyptian or Canaanite literature, which is curious in view of the great influence of both on the religion and literature of Israel. On the other hand, the similarities between the Mesopotamian and Hebrew stories are marked. It is unlikely that Israel borrowed the conceptions during the Assyrian period (between the 9th and 7th centuries), since the Assyrians were a warlike rather than a cultured people, or during the Exile in Babylon (6th century), since the most important result of the Exile was the growing tendency of the Israelites to *separate* themselves from their Gentile captors. In fact, it seems most probable that some of the traditions about the Creation, the Garden of Eden, the Flood, the stories of Nimrod (Gen. 10. 8 ff.), and of the Tower of Babel (Gen. 11) were brought from Mesopotamia by the patriarchs themselves. Indeed, the story of the Tower of Babel must have originated at a time when Babylon and its great temple-tower or *ziggurat* were flourishing and well known: that is, at latest between 1800 and 1600 B.C. before the city was destroyed by the Hittites, though the *ziggurat* may have been erected as early as the 24th century B.C.

Best known of course is the story of the great flood which covered the earth and destroyed all life except that preserved by Noah in the Ark. That the Babylonians had a similar story has been known from ancient times. In 1872 George Smith announced his discovery of an older version which he had found in the library of Asshurbanapal uncovered at Nineveh in 1853. Since that time we have learned that this version rests on still older sources which can be traced back to the 3rd millennium B.C.

The Babylonian flood is recounted in the Gilgamesh epic, a long poem about the ancient King of Uruk in southern Babylonia, who, in the course of his quest for eternal life, met Utnapishtim, the only mortal who had ever attained it. In the days of old, when the gods had decided to destroy mankind by a flood, Utnapishtim and his wife had been warned by the god Ea, had built a ship, and had saved themselves and pairs of living things. Afterwards the Storm, Enlil, repented of the flood and rewarded Utnapishtim with eternal life.

Many of the details of the Babylonian tale of the Flood are so close to the biblical story that the ultimate dependence of the latter upon the former seems clear. Not only the general outline of the story, but the building of the ship, the release of birds at the end of the flood, and the sacrifices of the flood-hero after the boat has landed on some mountains, are common to both accounts.

(Much has been written about the historicity of the Flood, particularly since the discovery of a 'flood' layer in the excavations of Ur in southern Babylonia by Sir Leonard Woolley in 1929. The confident assurance of this excavator that he had found evidence of the Flood has been enthusiastically shared in many popular handbooks since.

Unfortunately, the facts do not enable the student to be as confident. Woolley seems to have dug some five pits through the early strata of occupation at Ur, but in only two of them did he find deposits of water-borne debris. The logical inference is that the flood in question did not cover the whole city of Ur but only part of it, that is, it was only a local inundation of the Euphrates at flood tide. Furthermore, the site showed no break in occupation as a result of the flood, something we should expect if there had been a major catastrophe of more than purely local and temporary incidence.)

The biblical story of the Flood is based on a north Mesopotamian rather than a Babylonian version, for the mountains on which the Ark landed are the mountains of Ararat or Armenia, just north of Haran, whereas in the Babylonian story they were just east of Mesopotamia.

It is evident, therefore, that the archaeological data are in agreement with the biblical tradition that the original home of the patriarchs was in the area of Haran.

The Patriarchs in Canaan

The patriarchs are represented in Genesis as making their living from their herds of cattle and their flocks of sheep and goats, wandering in the hill country of Palestine between Dothan and Beersheba, and constantly concerned about pasturage and springs, for the latter especially were none too plentiful in a country in which the surface rock is a soft and absorbent limestone. They were not primarily peasants, therefore, but nomads. That this did not mean that their style of life was 'primitive' is shown by the contemporary Egyptian story (*c.* 1900 B.C.) of Sinuhe, a high official in the Egyptian Government, who had to flee the country for reasons of state. He took refuge with an Amorite chieftain in Syria, and commented very favorably on the way he was entertained. The story incidentally reveals that there were close relations between Egypt and Syria–Palestine at the time, and makes the story of Abraham's visit to Egypt (Gen. 12) quite credible. A contemporary Egyptian relief (*c.* 1900 B.C.) depicts a family of Semitic semi-nomads entering Egypt, and probably indicates fairly closely how we should envisage the patriarchal family.

The tradition associates each of the patriarchs with a certain area of the Palestinian hill country: Abraham with Mamre, south of Jerusalem (Gen. 13. 18), the site of the cave of Machpelah, the patriarchal burial-chamber (Gen. 23. 17); Isaac with Beersheba (Gen. 26. 23; 28. 10); Jacob with Bethel, Shechem and Dothan (33. 18; 35. 1; 37. 17). At all these sites there were apparently old holy places, where altars and pillars were set up by Abraham and Jacob for the purposes of worship. Archaeological evidence confirms that these towns were the main settlements in the area between 2000 and 1700 B.C. Dothan, Shechem, and Bethel were all in existence. The wells at Beersheba are certainly very ancient. Hebron, we are told in Num. 13. 22, was founded 'seven years before Zoan in Egypt'. Zoan was a city in the Nile Delta which had a number of names in its history, probably including that of Raamses, the store city built or rebuilt by the Hebrews in bondage (Ex. 1. 11). It has been excavated and is known to have been rebuilt by the Hyksos about 1700 B.C. Hebron, therefore, having been founded about the same time, probably under the name of Kiriath-arba (Gen. 23. 2; 35. 27), was evidently not in existence in the time of Abraham, a fact which accounts for the association of the patriarch rather with Mamre, in the same vicinity.

We do not know a great deal about the Canaanites, who are said to have been in the land at the time, except what we can learn from the material remains in their cities. During the period just before and after 2000 B.C. there would appear to have been little urban activity in Palestine, whereas during the 19th century a whole new era began (Middle Bronze II); the number of towns increased and the quality of the material culture improved rapidly. Some Egyptian figurines and pieces of pottery have been found which list Asiatic enemies of Egypt during this age. The Berlin texts (20th century B.C.) give evidence that Palestine was in a nomadic or semi-nomadic state at the time, the only Palestinian cities mentioned being Jerusalem and Ashkelon. The Brussels texts (late 19th century) reflect the increased urban activity, mentioning many cities and their kings.

One of the great Canaanite cities of the country at this time was Gezer, situated on one of the foothills bordering the coastal plain south-east of Jaffa. It was guarded by a very strong city wall, and seems to have been an Egyptian outpost about 1900 B.C., to judge from the statues and other objects found there. At a second great city, Megiddo, guardian of the pass through Mount Carmel from the Plain of Sharon to the Esdraelon Plain, further Egyptian objects have been discovered, and also a series of three temples, all of the same shape, which were presumably the 'houses' of three different deities. The 'high place' of this period found at Megiddo has been mentioned in Chapter I.

A third flourishing area was the Jordan Valley. Genesis speaks about the favored situation of 'the cities of the Plain' (Gen. 13. 10) and subsequently describes their destruction (Gen. 19. 24–28). 'Brimstone and fire' might suggest volcanic eruption, but since there are no volcanoes, we are probably to think in terms of an earthquake, such disturbances being not uncommon in the Rift Valley. A thorough survey of southern Transjordan east and south of the Dead Sea has shown that the village settlements which had sprung up before 2000 B.C. were suddenly abandoned in the 20th or 19th century, and that the people apparently returned to nomadic pursuits. The cities Sodom, Gomorrah, and Zoar have not been found, because they are in all probability beneath the shallow waters at the southern tip of the Dead Sea. The date which these discoveries supply for Abraham, assuming that he was contemporary with the fall of the cities of the Plain, namely, the 20th or 19th century B.C., fits in with the late biblical tradition that Abraham left Mesopotamia a little more than 600 years before the Exodus from Egypt. This date for Abraham is, however, extremely tentative, and some scholars prefer a date some centuries later.[1]

In Gen. 14 we have an old story of the raid by four Mesopotamian kings into Transjordan and the defeat and plunder of the cities of the Plain. The route taken by these kings is an old road through Transjordan, called by later Israelites 'the King's Highway' (Num. 20. 17; 21. 22). One of these kings, Amraphel, used to be identified with the great Babylonian king Hammurabi, but this is no longer tenable. None of the kings can with certainty be identified at present. The reason for the raid may well have been the copper mines south of the Dead Sea, for these were being worked and explain the prosperity of the villages before they were suddenly and mysteriously abandoned.

Family burial caves are now well known to us through excavations. The story of Abraham's purchase of such a cave at Mamre from Ephron the Hittite (Gen. 23) has recently been studied in the light of Hittite law.[2] The Hittite code of laws, found at Boghazköy in Turkey, specifies that if a buyer purchases all the seller's property he must render certain feudal services, and that the transfer of the land involves the transfer of the duties. This explains why Ephron was so anxious to part with the field as well as the cave.

The significance of the setting up of pillars by Jacob (Gen. 28. 18 ff.; 31. 44 ff.; 33. 20, reading 'pillar' instead of 'altar') is not entirely clear, though many such pillars have been discovered. They appear to have been erected chiefly as memorial stones to commemorate a theophany, a vow or sacred covenant rite, or even an ancestor or important official.

[1] See H. H. Rowley, *From Joseph to Joshua* (London, 1950); Cyrus H. Gordon, *Introduction to Old Testament Times* (Ventnor, N.J., 1953).
[2] Manfred R. Lehmann, *BASOR* 129 (February 1953), pp. 15–18.

The patriarchal family deity was known as 'the God of the Fathers' or 'the God of Abraham, Isaac and Jacob'. Pagan antiquity provided many illustrations [1] of this type of family deity, whom a patriarch would consciously choose as his personal God and with whom he would enter a special contractual or covenantal relationship. This deity took special charge of the family or clan, and successive generations would choose and enter into the relationship anew. In all probability we have here one portion of the background of the later covenant between God and Israel. 'The God of the Fathers' was identified with Yahweh (Ex. 3); he became Israel's God, and Israel by free choice became his people. The proper name of the patriarchal deity is not known with certainty, but one of his titles has been preserved. It is 'Shaddai' (Gen. 17. 1; Ex. 6. 3), a Mesopotamian word meaning 'mountaineer', and thus pointing to the might and awe-inspiring majesty of the deity. Abraham's worship of El Elyon ('God Most High') in Jerusalem (Gen. 14) shows that the patriarchs were not monotheists, however. El was the head of both the 'Amorite' and later Canaanite pantheon of deities, and we have no reason to suppose that he is anything else in the original tradition behind Gen. 14.

Maps, Texts, and Illustrations

Maps

WHA, Plates II, IV, XVIII; Grollenberg, Maps 1–6

Texts

(p. 22) The Mari Texts: *ANE*, 260–2; *ANET*, 482–3
(p. 24) The Nuzi Texts: *ANET*, 219–20

[1] See A. Alt, *Der Gott der Väter* (Leipzig, 1929); J. Lewy, *RHR* CX (1934), pp. 29–65, esp. pp. 50 ff.

(p. 26) The Babylonian Flood Story: *ANE*, 40–75; *ANET*, 72–99; *DOTT*, 17–26

(p. 26) Sumerian precursor of the Flood Story: *ANE*, 28–30; *ANET*, 42–4

(p. 28) The story of Sinuhe: *ANE*, 5–11; *ANET*, 18–22

(p. 29) The Berlin Texts: *ANE*, 225–6; *ANET*, 328–9

Illustrations (The references are to Figures)

(p. 22) Excavations at Mari: Grollenberg, 5, 112–20

(p. 24) The Nuzi Texts: Wright, 17; *WHA*, 17

(p. 25) *Teraphim*: Wright, 18

(p. 26) Ziggurats: *ANE*, 188–90; *ANEP*, Index, s.v. 'ziggurat'; Grollenberg, 86–7; Wright, 16; *WHA*, 11; Wiseman, 18–19

(p. 26) The Babylonian Flood Story: *ANE*, 69; *ANEP*, 248; *DOTT*, 1; Wiseman, 10

(p. 28) The Beni-Hasan Relief: *ANE*, 2; *ANEP*, 3; Grollenberg, 121; Wiseman, 25; Wright, 19; *WHA*, 9

(p. 29) The Brussels Texts: *ANE*, 153; *ANEP*, 593; Wright, 21

(p. 30) Canaanite Megiddo: *ANE*, 186; *ANEP*, 708, 734–5; Wright, 23–4; *WHA* (5th ed.), 85

CHAPTER III

EXODUS AND CONQUEST

According to the Old Testament, the Exodus from Egyptian slavery was the dominating event in Israelite history and faith. Yet the events which were so important to Israel were so unimportant to the Egyptians that no record of them has been preserved outside the Bible. Nevertheless, the tradition must have a historical basis. One indication of this is the appearance in the biblical record of a number of Egyptian names. Moses itself, an abbreviated name, is from an Egyptian verb meaning 'to bear, beget'. In Egyptian names such as Thutmose and Rameses the first syllable is the name of a god, while *mose* or *meses* indicates that the god is the begetter of the person named. Other Egyptian names are Phinehas, Hophni, Pashhur, and perhaps Hur and Merari. The Egyptian names in the Joseph story (Potiphar, Potiphera, Asenath, Zaphenath-paneah) are, however, from a later period: it may be that the original Egyptian names were later modernized.

The Egyptian coloring in the story of the Sojourn is very good, and must have been given to it by those who knew Egypt well. Dreams were indeed regarded by Egyptians as significant when interpreted. The title given to Joseph by Potiphar (Gen. 39. 5) corresponds exactly to the known Egyptian title of the office described. The titles 'chief of the butlers' and 'chief of the bakers' (Gen. 40. 2) occur in Egyptian inscriptions. The birthday of Pharaoh is known to have been an occasion for feasting, and possibly for the release of prisoners (Gen. 40. 20 ff.). We know also that magicians were plentiful in Egypt (Gen. 41. 8), that 'every (Asiatic) shepherd is an abomination to the Egyptians' (46. 34: cf. also 43. 32); that Joseph's life-span of 110 years (50. 22) was considered the traditional length of a happy and prosperous life in Egyptian inscriptions; and that embalming or mummification (50. 2 f., 26) was the customary Egyptian preparation of the body of an important person for burial. Pharaoh's gifts to Joseph upon the latter's induction into high office (41. 42 f.) would be quite in keeping with Egyptian custom. It has also been pointed out that the ten plagues (Ex. 7–12) are based on natural scourges which are still troublesome in Egypt.

The story of Joseph may have attracted details from other popular stories. For example, the incident of Potiphar's wife (Gen. 39. 7 ff.) is paralleled by the Egyptian Tale of Two Brothers, in which the affectionate relation between the brothers Anubis and Bitis is disturbed by the attempt of Anubis' wife to seduce Bitis.

The Historical Background of the Sojourn

The position to which Joseph attained in Egypt is well illustrated by inscriptions and reliefs. From these Egyptian records we should judge that he combined in his person two offices: that of 'governor' or Prime Minister at the head of the government, and that of 'superintendent of the granaries'. The governor was minister of the interior and chief magistrate, and sometimes leader of public worship as well. The superintendent had to see to it that the grain supply, in which the wealth and stability of Egypt lay, was plentiful, and had to present to Pharaoh in solemn audience 'the account of the harvests'. If there had been 'a better harvest than for 30 years', then the official would be anointed and decked with necklaces. It was apparently not unusual for foreigners to rise to positions of authority in the New Empire (after 1570 B.C.), and it is possible that Joseph lived at a time when foreigners were ruling over Egypt, as we shall see.

Two Egyptian documents indicate that it was the customary thing for frontier officials to allow bedouin from Palestine and Sinai to enter Egypt during hard times and live in the Goshen area (cf. Gen. 46. 28 ff.). Goshen is not mentioned in the Egyptian records, but the alternative names 'the land of Rameses' (Gen. 47. 11) and 'the field of Zoan' (Ps. 78. 12) refer to a city in the eastern part of the Nile Delta—it was known by both names—which is frequently mentioned in Egyptian records. This region, now known as the region of the Wadi Tumilat, has remained up to modern times one of the richest areas of Egypt (Gen. 47. 11), and in the last century half its population was still nomadic. If there is any place in Egypt where the Hebrew shepherds should have settled, this is the region.

Many scholars place the entry of Joseph and his family into Egypt in the time of the Hyksos, or 'Rulers of Foreign Countries'. These were Asiatics who invaded Egypt shortly before 1700 B.C. and ruled over a great empire, including at least Palestine and southern Syria, for 150 years. Objects belonging to one of their greatest kings have been found as far away as Crete and Mesopotamia. Several Palestinian cities which were destroyed in the 16th century give evidence of the Egyptian campaign which followed the expulsion of the Hyksos from Egypt.

The Hyksos capital, Avaris, was probably located at San el-Hagar in the Delta, a site which is thought to have been named successively Avaris (before 1500 B.C.), Rameses

(1300–1100 B.C.), and finally Tanis or Zoan (after 1100 B.C.). Some of the Hyksos fortifications have been unearthed, and, more important, a *stele* or monument erected by an official of Rameses II to commemorate the 400th anniversary of the founding of the city by a Hyksos ruler. Since the date of the *stele* is 1320–1300 B.C., the city must have been founded 1720–1700 B.C. The tradition that Hebron was built seven years before Zoan (Tanis) in Egypt (Num. 13. 22) suggests that there were Hebrews in Egypt when the city was founded, i.e., in the Hyksos period. It must be stated, however, that some scholars do not accept the location of Rameses at Tanis, preferring Qantir, a few miles to the south, and that some are doubtful as to the interpretation and historical value of the '400-year *stele*'.

Another pointer to the Hyksos period is the impression that the land of Goshen was not far away from the Egyptian capital. The site of Avaris in the eastern Delta was used as the capital only by the Hyksos (about 1720–1580 B.C.) and by Pharaohs of the XIXth Dynasty (after 1300 B.C.). Before and after the Hyksos the capital was Thebes in Upper Egypt.

It is also possible that the story of Joseph's compulsory purchase of all the land for Pharaoh (Gen. 47. 13 ff.) may reflect a social revolution brought about by the Hyksos. Before their rule the land was largely owned by powerful nobles. After their expulsion, under the XVIIIth Dynasty, the land was administered by a bureaucracy, and the peasants were the serfs of the Pharaoh. It is not certain that the Hyksos were responsible, but it is to be noted that they brought about an equally great social upheaval in Palestine.

THE PHARAOH OF THE EXODUS

The book of Exodus begins by telling us that after the death of Joseph and his generation, the Hebrews in Egypt increased until they became a serious minority problem for the Pharaoh, who forced them to go to work on government building projects, including the store-cities of Pithom and Raamses (Ex. 1. 11).

We have already seen that on the borders of every civilized country in the Near East there were ever-shifting groups of nomadic peoples (*Hapiru*), who in times of peace worked in various capacities for the settled people. These figure in Egyptian texts as *'Apiru*, and some of them are represented as engaged in dragging up stone for temples built by Rameses II (1290–1224 B.C.). We shall see that it must have been in his reign that the cities of Pithom and Raamses were built by the Hebrews.

Pithom may be identified with the site Tell er-Retabeh (or Ertabeh) in the Wadi Tumilat. The finest structure on the site was the temple of Rameses II, and since no other royal building has been found there, the Israelites, if they worked there at all, must have done so in the time of Rameses II.

Raamses must have been the capital of Rameses II, named by him 'House of Rameses', which was situated in the eastern Delta, probably at Tanis. Since the site was deserted between the expulsion of the Hyksos and the time of Rameses II, and there is abundant evidence of the building operations of Rameses II, the Israelites must have worked there at least during the early part of his reign, if there is any historical value in the tradition at all. Thus Rameses II must have been the Pharaoh who figures in the story of the Exodus.

THE ROUTE OF THE EXODUS

In their Exodus from Egypt the Israelites avoided the direct but well-traveled and well-guarded commercial and military road to Canaan, 'the way of the land of the Philistines' (Ex. 13. 17). The long line of Egyptian fortifications along this route was described by Pharaoh Seti I in his Karnak inscription. Instead they chose 'the way of the wilderness by the Reed Sea' (Ex. 13. 18). This, and not 'Red Sea', is the correct rendering of the Hebrew *Yam Suph*, and it is highly improbable that we should identify it with the northern arm of the Red Sea known today as the Gulf of Suez. In the first place there are no reeds in the Red Sea. In the second place the biblical account implies that the Reed Sea was the barrier between Egyptian soil and the desert: if the Red Sea were meant, it would have been necessary to cross a considerable tract of desert to get to it. In a text describing the wonders of Rameses-Tanis, however, mention is made of a 'Papyrus Marsh' near the city, a name which immediately recalls the biblical 'Reed Sea'. Thus the crossing was made not far from Rameses. This is confirmed by the identification of Baal-zephon (Ex. 14. 2) with Tahpanhes, the modern Tell Defneh, in the same region, on the basis of a Phoenician letter which mentions the god 'Baal-zephon and all the gods of Tahpanhes'. The reference in the account of the Exodus will be to the town which contained the temple of this god.

The route which Israel followed across Sinai is not entirely clear, and scholars are not agreed as to where Mt. Sinai (or Mt. Horeb) was. The traditional site is among the granite mountains in the south of the Sinai peninsula, with the ancient copper and turquoise mines to which the Egyptians sent regular expeditions. A number of scholars believe that Mt. Sinai is to be located in ancient Midian, south-east of Edom in Arabia, on the ground that the account in Ex. 19 implies volcanic activity, and that this is the only area where such activity is known to have existed. Yet the account could equally well imply a mountain storm, and in any case the Old Testament frequently describes God's appearances in terms taken from awesome natural phenomena, so that it is impossible to use them as evidence for a precise geographical location. According to Deut. 1. 2, the journey from Kadesh-barnea to Mt. Horeb (Sinai) took eleven days, a tradition which may well have been derived from the time taken to traverse an old pilgrimage route. The stations along this route are perhaps preserved in Num. 33, and Elijah may well have followed it (1 Kings 19. 1–8). The traditional location of Mt. Sinai agrees with this route very well indeed. Furthermore, it is difficult to understand why the early Church should have located the sacred spot in the most inaccessible and dangerous area imaginable for pilgrims, unless the tradition was so old and firmly fixed that no debate was permitted about it. Finally, a few of the stations can be identified with some degree of probability along the route to the southern mountains of Sinai: thus Elim (Ex. 15. 27; Num. 33. 9) with the oasis of Wadi Gharandel, 63 miles from Suez; Dophkah (Num. 33. 12) with the Egyptian mining center at Serabit el-Khadem, because the name seems to mean 'smeltery'; Rephidim (Ex. 17. 1; Num. 33. 14) with Wadi Refayid; etc.

According to Israelite tradition, Moses married into the family of a Midianite priest, named Jethro in one source, Reuel in another (Ex. 2. 16 ff.; 18. 1 ff.). The family of Reuel's son, Hobab, subsequently became Israelite (Num. 10. 29; Jdg. 4. 11). This family was known as 'Kenite', a name which means 'smith'. There were copper mines east and south-east of the Gulf of Aqabah (Midian), in the Arabah (the valley south of the Dead Sea), and in the area of the traditional Mt. Sinai. These mines were worked far more intensively in ancient times than they are today, and must have provided the inhabitants of Midian and Sinai with a profitable livelihood. By 1500 B.C. the semi-nomadic smiths of the Sinai peninsula were using the earliest known alphabet, invented and developed by the Canaanites in Syria, and subsequently borrowed by both Israelites and Greeks. The smiths of Sinai and Midian must therefore be thought of as a prosperous people, in close commercial contact with Egypt and Palestine. The evidence for the theory that Yahweh was originally the tribal God of the Kenites or Midianites is, however, very tenuous.

The descriptions of the portable tent or Tabernacle, which was the focus of the Israelite encampment in the desert, and of the Ark of the Covenant, which was placed inside the tent, are the work of late priestly authors. However, the predominant use of acacia, goat's hair tent-cloth, ram-skins, and lamb-skins in the construction of the Tabernacle point to nomadic life and probably represent authentic tradition. The early Arabs, before the days of Mohammed, possessed portable sacred tents. Even in modern times certain Arabic tribes have been known to possess a portable object similar in function to the Ark. It is the visible focus of the various clans possessing it, because the god Allah is thought to live in it, and it is used as a palladium in battle (cf. Num. 10. 35 f.).

The census lists in Num. 1 and 26, probably variations of the same list, give the number of males involved in the Exodus and the Wandering as slightly over 600,000. With women and children the total population would be between two and three million. The Sinai peninsula could not possibly have supported this number. Three to five thousand would be a more reasonable figure. The army of Rameses II in the battle of Kadesh against the Hittites numbered 20,000 men, and would constitute no threat to an Israelite army of 600,000. It is possible that the lists represent a census taken in a later age, e.g., in the period of the Judges or in the time of David (2 Sam. 24), and that the word for 'thousand' in the list has a specialized military meaning.

The eventual entry into Palestine was made through Transjordan, where the tribes came into contact with the kingdoms of Edom and Moab. Transjordan was extensively explored by Nelson Glueck between 1930 and 1940. By examining hundreds of ancient sites and dating the time of their occupation by means of the fragments of pottery still to be found on them, he has been able to chart the boundaries of the ancient kingdoms of Ammon, Moab, and Edom. He has also discovered that they were not founded before the 13th century. For some 600 years before that the inhabitants had apparently led a nomadic existence and had not settled in towns. Then quite suddenly, between 1300 and 1100 B.C., towns sprang up all over southern Transjordan. As the kingdoms of Moab and Edom were already in existence at the time of the Conquest, it would appear that we have here another indication that the date of the Exodus could not be before the 13th century.

The activities of Balaam (Num. 22–24), whom Balak King of Moab brought from Pethor on the Upper Euphrates to curse Israel, are well illustrated by the activities of the Mesopotamian diviner or *baru*. The Babylonians developed elaborate methods of divining and predicting by omens of every conceivable kind. During the 2nd millennium this art and the diviners themselves spread everywhere; the personal seal of one of them has been found at Beth-shan in Palestine. Each detail of the story of Balaam follows what we know to have been the diviner's rules. The divination is carried out early in the morning, as the best results were thought to be obtained before sunrise. Three attempts were made: the number three played an important role in Babylonian magic. Perhaps Balaam's reason for suddenly giving up the divination (Num. 24. 1) was that he might lose his reputation as a diviner. The result was that Balak refused to pay the promised fee. The story is quite intelligible when Balaam is studied as a Babylonian *baru*.

The Conquest of Canaan

The view of the Conquest presented in the book of Joshua is that a long drawn-out struggle took place, but that ultimate success was possible only because of a successful initial campaign led by Joshua. This campaign was carried out in three phases: (1) the securing of a foothold in the central hill country, through the capture of Jericho and Ai, and through the Gibeonite alliance (Josh. 6–9); (2) the campaign in the south which avoided Jerusalem but took the rest of the territory later occupied by the tribe of Judah (Josh. 10); and (3) a campaign in Galilee, which, though successful in gaining territory, actually destroyed none of the fortified cities except Hazor (Josh. 11).

The impression given is that the whole country was completely subjugated. Judges 1, however, gives an entirely different picture. Instead of being a single united campaign under Joshua, the seizure of the land was a long process involving a series of struggles on the part of the individual tribes. In the past it has been assumed that the older material in Jdg. 1 is the more reliable, while the later account in Joshua must be regarded as exaggerated. But this view must be modified. The book of Joshua is well aware that Joshua's campaigns left much to be done (11. 13, 22; cf. Jdg. 2. 20–23; Deut. 7. 22) and in fact lists the areas still unconquered (Josh. 13). Furthermore, Jdg. 1 is not an old, unified account of the original Conquest, but a collection of miscellaneous fragments of varying date and reliability.

Archaeological evidence suggests that there was a major campaign in the 13th century, during which several important Canaanite city-states were brought to an end, and which allowed the Israelite tribes to settle, especially in the hill country; and that this was followed, in the 12th and 11th centuries, by a period of continual local struggle, since every town so far excavated was destroyed from one to four times, and yet few of the destructions can be correlated with each other. By the time of Israel's first king, Saul, only the central hill country and part of Transjordan had been occupied, since the invaders were not equipped to besiege such fortresses as Beth-shan, Taanach, and Megiddo in the Plain of Esdraelon, or Dor and Gezer, guarding ascents to the hill country along the coast (Jdg. 1. 27 ff.). The Israelites were no match for their enemies on the plains, where chariots could operate (Jdg. 1. 19; cf. 1 Kings 20. 23).

The Conquest in its Historical Setting

The first reference to Israel outside the Bible was made by the Pharaoh Merneptah about 1220 B.C. on a *stele* recording his victories. 'Israel' is a recognizable group living in Palestine, if not yet a settled nation. It has already been pointed out that if Israelites had any part in the building of Pithom and Raamses (Ex. 1. 11), some of them must have been still in Egypt during the early years of Rameses II (1290–1224). Consequently it is reasonable to suppose that the Exodus under Moses occurred some time during the first half of the 13th century.

The land of Canaan at this time was nominally an Egyptian province organized on the city-state system. Each city was ruled by a native 'governor', who was not interfered with as long as he paid tribute and raised labor forces for royal projects. Our most important source of information about Canaan during this era is a series of letters found in the archives of the palace of Pharaoh Amenophis IV (Akhnaton, *c.* 1377–1360 B.C.) at Tell el-Amarna in Egypt. These letters were written, for the most part, by Asiatic kings and officials to the Egyptian court. Those from Canaan reveal a chaotic state of plot and counterplot, and are full of contradictory accusations. A number of the letters complain about the *Hapiru* or *'Apiru* (for the connection of this word with 'Hebrew' see pp. 23 f., 38 above), and in the past the references have been taken to imply that a great invasion from the desert was taking place, connected in some way with the Hebrew conquest of Palestine. It is now thought, however, that the *'Apiru* were not invaders but lawless gangs within Canaan, composed partly of mercenaries and partly of members of the oppressed population. Local kings even apply the name to neighboring kings and their armies who were seizing land and towns, while those so named write to Pharaoh protesting their loyalty.

Another reason for not connecting the Israelite conquest with the Amarna period is that of the nine city-states in southern Palestine mentioned in Josh. 10–12 only four (Gezer, Jerusalem, Lachish, and [probably] Hebron) existed about 1375 B.C. The city wall of Debir (the modern

Tell Beit Mirsim) was not erected before the latter part of the 14th century. The Conquest belongs to the 13th century, by which time the power of the large older city-states had been reduced, and the number of such states increased.

Israel obtained its foothold in Canaan in the central hill country of western Palestine and in Gilead across the Jordan, neither of which was a center of settled civilization. It is curious, therefore, that nothing is said about a conquest of central Palestine in the book of Joshua, especially as the region was an important one in subsequent Israelite history. Joshua himself figures in the covenant ceremonies at Shechem, the capital of the region in early times, at which all the tribes gathered (Josh. 8. 30–35; 24). The explanation, according to most scholars, is that Shechem at that time was controlled by Hebrews who had either never been in Egypt, and therefore did not take part in the Exodus, or else had been part of an earlier Exodus. Perhaps they were part of the Hyksos movement, and settled in the area when the Hyksos were driven out of Egypt about 1550 B.C. It is possible that the differences between Judah and Israel in later times had their origin here. Certainly we know from the Tell el-Amarna letters that a century before Joshua the Shechem area was in the control of people who paid scant respect to Pharaoh and their neighbors. The king, Lab-'ayu, quoted an old Canaanite proverb in a letter to Pharaoh: 'If even ants are smitten, they do not accept it (passively) but they bite the hand of the man who smites them.' It has also long been recognized that Gen. 34 embodies a tradition of an early Hebrew relationship with Shechem which was not necessarily altered by the Sojourn and Exodus. The tradition of Josh. 24, in which Joshua seals the covenant with a united Israel at a city he has not had to conquer, would be explicable if there were already a mixed Canaanite–Hebrew group of clans at Shechem, united by covenant, and preserving the memory of a relationship with the Israelite movement.

THE FALL OF JERICHO

Squarely in the path of any invader of the hill country from the southern portion of the Jordan valley lay the fortress of Jericho. The Israelite tradition was that God caused the walls of the city to fall down after the Israelites had marched round it for seven days (Josh. 6). Interest in the excavations has naturally centered on the light they might shed on this tradition.

The first excavators were the Germans Sellin and Watzinger (1908–10). The British expedition under Professor John Garstang (1930–36) made very important discoveries. It was learned that the town was founded in the latter part of the Stone Age before the invention of pottery; this made it the oldest town in Palestine to be excavated so far. Garstang also made discoveries about the fortifications of the city at different periods: in particular, two brick walls which he assigned to the 15th century had been violently destroyed, and the town had been set on fire. From the latest pottery found on the site Garstang concluded that the city had been finally destroyed not later than 1385 B.C.

The joint British and American expedition under Miss Kathleen Kenyon (1952–58) has been very successful in reconstructing the history of Stone Age Jericho. But it has also been learnt that the two walls which Garstang assigned to the 15th century are not contemporary with each other, and that the destruction of which he found such striking evidence took place at least a thousand years earlier than he thought. In fact, thanks to the processes of erosion, virtually nothing remains of the last period of occupation, between 1500 and 1200 B.C. Thus Jericho provides no evidence either for the manner or for the precise date of its fall to the Israelites.

The Fall of Bethel-Ai

According to the biblical story, the first city to be taken in the hill country proper by Joshua was Ai, which was thereupon burned and 'made a tell (mound of ruins) for ever' (Josh. 8. 28). Excavations have shown, however, that Ai, a flourishing Canaanite city between about 3200 and 2400 B.C., with great walls and a fine temple, was entirely destroyed about 2400 B.C. and never again inhabited, except by a few Israelites about 1000 B.C. That means that the city had been in ruins for about a thousand years before the Conquest. How, then, are we to explain the story in the Bible?

Three main theories have been presented: (1) that the story was entirely invented at a later date to explain the presence of the ruin; (2) that Ai was temporarily occupied by the people of Bethel, a mile and a half away; this would not, however, explain the references to the 'king of Ai' in Josh. 8; (3) that the story of the conquest of Bethel was transferred at a later time to the old 'Ruin' (Ai) to explain the latter's existence. The book of Joshua does not contain a story of the capture of Bethel, though the memory of its destruction is preserved (Jdg. 1. 22–26; cf. Josh. 12. 16). The excavations at Bethel directed by Professor Albright in 1934 showed that Bethel was destroyed by a great fire some time in the 13th century. The Canaanite city destroyed was a fine one, with excellent houses, paved or plastered floors, and drains. The next town on the site was much poorer. The break between the two is so complete that there can be no doubt that this was the Israelite destruction.

THE CAMPAIGNS IN JUDAH AND GALILEE

Josh. 10 describes the campaign in which Joshua took the territory later occupied by Judah, while avoiding the strong city-states of Jerusalem and Gezer. All the cities mentioned except Makkedah can now be located with a high degree of probability, and several of them provide evidence that such a campaign was carried out.

The ruins of Lachish, for example, have been discovered at the modern Tell ed-Duweir, which was excavated by a British expedition under J. L. Starkey (1932–38). Like Bethel, the city was destroyed during the 13th century. A bowl was discovered in the burnt debris on which an Egyptian tax collector had recorded deliveries of wheat from local harvests, in the fourth year of a certain Pharaoh, whose name is not given. Specialists in Egyptian say that the writing on the bowl is to be dated about the time of Pharaoh Merneptah (1224–1216 B.C.). The bowl must therefore be dated in the time of Merneptah, or possibly in the time of a successor who reigned four years or more—at any rate in the last two decades of the 13th century. The bowl was broken in the destruction of the city, and was probably not very old when broken, so that Lachish must have fallen to Israel between 1220 and 1200 B.C.

We are told that the only fortified city that Joshua destroyed in Galilee was Hazor (Josh. 11. 10–13). The location of this city was fixed in 1926 at Tell el-Qedah, ten miles north of the Sea of Galilee, on the highway leading from Egypt through Palestine to Syria, Asia Minor, and Mesopotamia. The mound is one of the largest in Palestine. Just to the north of it is a huge rectangular plateau, protected in places by a wall and on the western side by a dry moat: this was probably a compound for the horse and chariot army of the Hyksos. An Israeli expedition under General Yigael Yadin (1955–58) discovered that the last Canaanite city had occupied not only the mound but the great enclosure also. With an estimated population of 40,000 living within an area of some 175 acres, Hazor was indeed one of the great cities of Syria–Palestine (cf. Josh. 11. 10). It was violently destroyed during the course of the 13th century, and thereafter the enclosure was more or less deserted and the occupation confined to the mound. In other words, the evidence for Joshua's destruction may well have been found, if the end of the Bronze Age city may be correlated with the Judaean campaign.

Conclusions

The evidence for the destruction suffered by Bethel, Lachish, and other cities during the 13th century certainly suggests that a campaign such as that depicted in Josh. 10 was carried out. It was in this period that a portion at least of the later nation of Israel gained entrance to Palestine.

There are still unsolved problems, of course, among them Jericho, Ai, and Shechem. Also, certain indications of chronology in the Old Testament do not harmonize with the 13th-century date for the Exodus and Conquest which archaeology has made virtually certain. 1 Kings 6. 1 says that Solomon began to build the Temple 480 years after the Exodus, in the fourth year of his reign, which was 959 B.C. according to the latest studies of the biblical chronology. This would make 1439 B.C. the date of the Exodus. It is thought, however, that the figure of 480 years is arrived at by assuming the traditional twelve generations between the Exodus and the time of Solomon to be of exactly forty years each. If the actual length of a generation was nearer twenty-five years than forty, then twelve generations back from Solomon would place the Exodus somewhere about the third quarter of the 13th century B.C., which would tally with the archaeological evidence.

In Ex. 12. 40 we are told that the children of Israel were in Egypt for 430 years. If the Exodus occurred early in the 13th century Joseph and his family would have been in Egypt about 1700 B.C., that is in the very days when the Hyksos were getting control of the country. This is the time when most scholars believe that the entry into Egypt would have taken place.

In Jdg. 11. 26 Jephthah tells the Ammonite king that Israel has been in possession of its Transjordanian territory for three hundred years. If Jephthah is dated in the 11th century B.C. the conquest of Transjordan would be pushed back into the 14th century. It is possible, however, that the figure of 300 years is artificially derived from the chronology of the book of Judges, because the addition of the years ruled by the successive judges and the intervening oppressions up to Jephthah's time gives a figure of 319 years. This chronology is suspect, because some of the judges and the oppressions were contemporary and not successive as the book presents them.

Maps, Texts, and Illustrations

Maps

WHA, Plates III–V, XVIII; Grollenberg, Maps 8–14

Texts

(p. 35) The Tale of Two Brothers: *ANE*, 12–16; *ANET*, 23–5; *DOTT*, 168–71

(p. 36) A frontier official's report: *ANE*, 183–4; *ANET*, 259

(p. 37) The 400 year *stele*: *ANET*, 252–3

(p. 39) The inscription of Seti I: *ANET*, 254–5

(p. 39) The description of Rameses-Tanis: *ANE*, 258–9; *ANET*, 470–1

(p. 44) The Israel *stele* of Merneptah: *ANE*, 231; *ANET*, 376–8; *DOTT*, 137–41

(p. 45) The Tell el-Amarna Letters: *ANE*, 262–76; *ANET*, 483–90; *DOTT*, 38–45

Illustrations (The references are to Figures)

(p. 38) Asiatic captives making bricks: Grollenberg, 132; *WHA*, 22

(p. 39) Mount Sinai: Grollenberg, 147–50; Wright, 33–4; *WHA*, 23

(p. 44) The Israel *stele*: *ANE*, 96; *ANEP*, 342–3; Grollenberg, 131; *DOTT*, 8; Wiseman, 40; Wright, 38

(p. 45) The Tell el-Amarna tablets: *ANEP*, 245; Wiseman, 115

(p. 46) Shechem: Grollenberg, 95–6, 100–1; *WHA*, 6

(p. 47) Jericho: Grollenberg, 38; *WHA* (5th ed.), 86

(p. 49) Canaanite Lachish: Wright, 47–8

(p. 49) Canaanite Hazor: Wright, 29

CHAPTER IV

THE PERIOD OF THE JUDGES

DURING the 13th and 12th centuries B.C. a series of events in the Near East brought the 'Bronze Age' to an end and ushered in the 'Iron Age'. While copper and bronze continue to be used as the most common metals, iron soon appears by their side in sufficient amount to introduce notable changes in architecture, shipbuilding, weapons, and especially agriculture.

The events were a series of invasions and a decline of power in Egypt, Mesopotamia, and Asia Minor which left Syria–Palestine largely free of outside domination for the first time in centuries. Barbarian invasions brought to an end the Hittite empire in Asia Minor and forced many Hittites to flee to, or remain in, northern Syria, where they soon dominated the cultural life as they had been dominating the political life during the preceding two centuries. By the middle of the 12th century the Egyptian Government was unable any longer to control Palestine and southern Syria. Except for a brief period under Tiglath-pileser I (*c.* 1116–1078 B.C.), Assyria was unable to maintain an extensive empire. Meanwhile Palestine was troubled by a number of invasions. The kingdoms of Edom, Moab, Sihon, and Og were set up in Transjordan in the 13th century. The last two were displaced by the Israelites, who then crossed the Jordan to seize most of Palestine's central ridge. During the 12th century eastern

Syria was overrun by the Aramaeans (the 'Syrians' of the English Biblc). The Ammonites probably established themselves across the Jordan in the same period. The so-called 'Sea Peoples,' displaced people from the Greek world, destroyed a number of cities along the Syro-Palestinian coast, including Ugarit (Ras Shamra), Sidon, and Tyre, and then attacked Egypt unsuccessfully. A large group of them, the Pelast (Philistines), seized and settled the Mediterranean coast between Joppa and Gaza, and subsequently gave their name to this region (Philistia) and ultimately to the whole land (Palestine). They organized themselves around five principal cities (Gaza, Ashkelon, Ashdod, Ekron, Gath), each ruled by an independent 'Lord' or 'Tyrant' after the Aegean model, though they acted together when occasion demanded. The Egyptian story of Wenamon mentions the Tjikal (perhaps people from Sicily, who are called 'Sikel' in Homer's *Odyssey*), another group of the 'Sea Peoples' who were settled at Dor, the chief city of the Plain of Sharon, about 1100 B.C.

The Canaanites were left in control of the sea-coast west of the Lebanon mountains and of a number of towns in Palestine, which were gradually conquered. Meanwhile a new state emerged in the north with its capital at Tyre, which began expanding into the Mediterranean by means of trade in the 10th century. Colonies were established in Cyprus; trading expeditions were sent into the western Mediterranean; and during the 9th century one of their mining colonies (probably called Tarshish) existed on Sardinia, as we know from Canaanite inscriptions found on the island. The Greeks called the new state Phoenicia, and by 800 B.C. had borrowed its alphabet.

Israel's Period of the Judges

During the 12th and most of the 11th centuries Israel was consolidating her position along Palestine's central ridge, and engaged in constant struggles against invaders and the remaining Canaanite city-states. The excavations suggest that it was a time of anarchy when no strong central government existed to impose peace. Bethel was destroyed four times during these two centuries. A number of Israelite towns were destroyed round about 1050 B.C., presumably by the Philistines. Megiddo suffered repeated troubles between the destruction of its great Canaanite fortifications and palace during the later 12th century and its complete rebuilding by David and Solomon in the 10th century.

There was a striking difference in political organization between Israel and the surrounding peoples at this time. While Edom, Moab, and Ammon were monarchies, and the Canaanite cities (Jerusalem, Gezer, Megiddo, Taanach, Beth-shan) remained organized as city-states, each with its own king, Israel was only a loose confederation of tribes, held together by no central political figure, but by a religious bond or 'covenant', the material symbol of which was the Ark of the Covenant in the central sanctuary at Shiloh. To defend themselves the Israelites depended on a spontaneous leadership which would arise when needed. In time, however, pressure, especially from the Philistines, became too strong, and a centralized government became a necessity.

It has been pointed out[1] that there are late parallels from other Mediterranean lands for the tribal organization

[1] M. Noth, *Das System der zwölf Stämme Israels* (Stuttgart, 1930); A. Alt, *Die Staatenbildung der Israeliten in Palästina* (Leipzig, 1930).

of Israel and its grouping around a central shrine. The classical writers tell us of a number of such amphictyonies from Greece and Italy, some definitely said to have had twelve tribes. One of their chief characteristics was the central sanctuary, forming a religious bond whereby the tribes were held together politically. Other very important comparative treatments of the Israelite covenant are those of Johannes Pedersen,[1] who interpreted it in terms of modern bedouin covenants in Arabia, and especially of Professor George E. Mendenhall,[2] who has discovered remarkably close and illuminating parallels in the international treaties of Western Asia during the 2nd millennium B.C.

These treaties were of two types: the parity treaty between equals, and the suzerainty treaty between a great king and a vassal. It is the latter which presents the most striking parallels, since the role of suzerain, claiming authority over other rulers, is precisely that assumed by the God of Israel. Six elements may be distinguished in these treaties:

(1) The identification of the Great King: 'Thus says X, the Great King . . .' This recalls the early covenant passages of the Old Testament, in which God speaks in the first person: 'I am the Lord' (Ex. 20. 1–2) or 'Thus says the Lord, the God of Israel' (Josh. 24. 2).

(2) A detailed presentation of the historical background to the relations between the Great King and the vassal which emphasizes particularly the benevolent actions of the former. In the Old Testament also the law

[1] *Israel* I–II (Copenhagen and London, 1926), Introduction and Part II; *Der Eid bei den Semiten* (Strasbourg, 1914).

[2] *BA*, XVII, No. 3 (September 1954); reprinted in *Law and Covenant in Israel and the Ancient Near East.*

is preceded by the historical description of what God has done for his people (see especially the covenant ceremony in Josh. 24. 2–13).

(3) The stipulations of the covenant, which are a description of the vassal's obligations. Among them there is always the prohibition against the vassal's engaging in relations with foreign powers, which reminds us of the First Commandment to Israel, which prohibits any relations with other deities (Ex. 20. 3; cf. 34. 13; Josh. 24. 14). The Great King left the internal relations of a vassal king with his people undisturbed. Similarly, in Israel the Ten Commandments established religious obligation, but they allowed considerable freedom in the conduct of civil life. The stipulations for civil law which we find, for example, in the 'Book of the Covenant' (Ex. 21–23) were originally examples of legal procedure written down for information and codified so that tribal differences in common law could be eliminated. Only later was this common law used to enforce morality.

(4) The stipulation that the document should be deposited in the sanctuary of the vassal and publicly read at regular intervals. We find similar provisions in Israel (Josh. 24. 26; Deut. 31. 9–13).

(5) The invocation of the deities of the respective parties as witnesses to the covenant. In Israel such witnesses are, of course, lacking.

(6) The blessings and curses which will attend the keeping or violation of the covenant. Whether the oldest Israelite covenants contained similar formulas we do not know, but the 'Book of the Covenant', the 'Holiness Code', and the Deuteronomic law all do so (Ex. 23. 20–33; Lev. 26; Deut. 27–28; cf. Josh. 8. 34).

It seems highly probable, therefore, that Israelite faith was given a framework borrowed and adapted from these international treaties. By its means the people were enabled to interpret their life in terms of loyalty to the Lord who had done so much for them and bound himself to them by solemn pact, and also to view sin as disloyalty and rebellion. It also suggests the background to so many of the common words in the Israelite religious vocabulary which we know to have been taken over from the realm of law.

The history of Israel's shrine at Shiloh during the period of the Judges can be reconstructed from the Old Testament records and from excavations by Danish scholars in 1926 and 1929. After the conquest was completed, the tabernacle was moved there from Gilgal (Josh. 18. 1). During the first half of the 11th century Eli was the priest in charge, and Samuel was trained there (1 Sam. 1 ff.). About 1050 B.C., after Israel's defeat by the Philistines at Ebenezer (1 Sam. 4), Shiloh was apparently destroyed (Jer. 7. 12 ff.; 26. 6 ff.). The archaeological evidence supports this. For the next thirty years Israel had to submit to Philistine domination, while the Ark remained at Kiriath-jearim, feared by Philistines and Israelites alike.

Archaeological Evidence for the Philistines

The Philistine cities of the southern coastal plain yield large quantities of a distinctive pottery. Its fine well-baked clay, its particular shapes, and its decoration, especially its spirals and birds, are readily distinguished. Its models are well known in the Greek world from which the Philistines are known to have come.

The economic stranglehold which the Philistines had over Israel when Saul became king is illustrated by 1 Sam. 13. 19–22.

> Now there was no smith found throughout all the land of Israel because the Philistines said: '(There must be none) lest the Hebrews make swords or spears.' But all the Israelites went down to the Philistines for each man to sharpen his plowpoint, and his axe, and his adze, and his mattock(?). And the price was a *pim* (2/3 of a shekel) for the plowpoints and for the axes and a third of a shekel for sharpening the adzes and for setting the goads (?-or, fixing the hafts?). So it came to pass on the day of battle, that neither sword nor spear were to be found in the hand of any of the people which were with Saul and Jonathan. . . .

The meaning of verse 21 was formerly obscure, especially because the word *pim* was unknown. Little weights with this word inscribed on them have turned up in the excavations, however, and the general sense is now clear, although some of the names for the agricultural implements are uncertain. Here we are told that the Philistines held such a control over Israel that they would permit no smith in the hill country in order that the Israelites should not stock the supplies of war. The farmers were forced to go down to Philistia to sharpen their tools, and were charged exorbitant prices for the service.

There is probably even more to be inferred from the passage. The metal in common use for tools and weapons since 4000 B.C. had been copper, or copper mixed with tin to form the harder bronze. Iron was not introduced into common use until after 1200 B.C. The secrets of the rather complicated smelting process seem to have been jealously guarded by the Hittites. The Israelites were hindered in building, agriculture, and conquest (Josh. 17. 16; Jdg. 1. 19) for lack of this important metal. Iron appears in Philistine tombs, but the earliest iron implement found in the hill country is a plowpoint from Saul's fortress at Gibeah (*c.* 1010 B.C.). It is a safe assumption that the metal was introduced into Palestine by the Philistines, who held a 'corner' on the iron market and closely guarded the trade secrets of its production. It was only after the first kings of Israel, Saul and David, had broken the Philistine power that the metal came into use in Israel, promptly effecting an economic revolution.

Canaanite Cities

The Philistines, then, were the most dangerous oppressors of Israel during the period of the Judges, furnishing the occasion for great exploits which were later celebrated in song and story, most notably those of Samson and of David versus Goliath. There were other oppressors, however, among them the group of Midianites or Arabians who made a raid against northern Palestine up the Jezreel valley and were met and routed by Gideon. This raid is particularly interesting, since it was, as far as we now know, the first time that camels were extensively used. Ancient reliefs and documents indicate that the camel, so widely used in the Near East today, had not been domesticated on any large scale before this time, probably because it is such a difficult and ill-tempered beast to handle. Ancient nomads, with their donkeys, sheep, and goats, could never move far from water. With the domestication of the camel the nomad was able to cover great distances and to live in areas where the shepherd could not exist.

Not least among the oppressors, however, were the Canaanites, whom the Israelites were only able gradually to subdue. Before 1200 B.C. control of most of the hill country had been wrested from them, but strong cities in the plain areas, where chariots could manoeuvre, held out for some time. Typical of these cities were Megiddo and Beth-shan in the north. The early 12th century palace of the Canaanite king at Megiddo was far more elaborate than that of any wealthy Israelite of later times, and in all probability was as large and substantial as that of Solomon. In it the excavators found a large number of gold, ivory, and alabaster objects which vividly illustrate the comparative wealth and culture of the Canaanite king. The ivories are typical Canaanite workmanship, mostly used for inlay on boxes, furniture, and the cedar walls of 'drawing-rooms'. The exact cause of the city's destruction during the third quarter of the 12th century is unknown. It is probably during the period when the city lay in ruins and before it was settled again that we are to date the events described in the Song of Deborah in Jdg. 5, which took place in the ancient battle area near Megiddo. This would explain why the battleground is further identified as being at Taanach, some 4 miles to the south-east, which would then have been the nearest town (Jdg. 5. 19).

Beth-shan was another strong fortress-city in the Jordan valley to the east of Megiddo, guarding the Vale of Jezreel, which led up from the Jordan into the great plain of Esdraelon. For three centuries the Egyptians had attempted to control this area, guarding the approaches through Palestine. In fact, Esdraelon had been one of the private granaries of the Pharaoh. During the early 12th century Rameses III, trying desperately to re-establish the Asiatic empire of his forefathers, rebuilt Beth-shan as a frontier post, but by the third quarter of the 12th century Egyptian control over Palestine had ceased.

During the 11th century Beth-shan was rebuilt, and probably by the Philistines. The city's temples (1 Sam. 31.

10; 1 Chr. 10. 10) have been excavated, and have been mentioned in connection with Canaanite religion. Beth-shan finally fell to Israel in the 10th century, as the excavations show, probably in the time of David.

The First Prophets

In 1 Sam. 10. 5 we hear for the first time of an organized group of 'prophets', men whose inspiration led them to ecstatic utterance (cf. Num. 11. 24–29). We are certainly not to think of ecstasy as a specifically Israelite phenomenon; it has appeared in many different religious. Indeed, its entry into Israel may well have been under foreign inspiration. In the Egyptian story of Wenamon (*c.* 1100 B.C.) the author tells us that while the prince of the Phoenician city of Byblos 'was making offering to his gods, the god seized one of his youths and made him possessed'. We are told that the Egyptian sign for the word 'possessed' shows a human figure in violent motion or epileptic convulsion. The Byblian king seems to have interpreted the event as a sign that the Egyptian god, Amon, had actually come to Byblos.

In Israel, however, ecstasy did not remain the chief or distinguishing mark of prophecy. The prophet was characteristically God's herald, sent to deliver a message; hence he customarily began his address: 'Thus saith the Lord.' When attacked, his defense could only be: 'The Lord has sent me' (cf. Jer. 26. 2, 15; 28. 15). Until recently, the prophetic office in this sense had appeared to be unique in Israel. In the archives of the city of Mari on the upper Euphrates, however, some interesting parallels have been unearthed from *c.* 1700 B.C.[1] Royal officials writing to the

[1] See A. Lods, in *Studies in Old Testament Prophecy*, ed. H. H. Rowley (Edinburgh, 1950), pp. 103–110; *Archives Royales de Mari*, ed. A. Parrot et G. Dossin, II (Paris, 1950), Letter No. 90; III (Paris, 1948), Letter No. 40; M. Noth, *BJRL*, 32 (1950), pp. 194–206.

king of Mari occasionally report to him that a man of such-and-such a god had come with a message for the king. He claimed that the god had sent him and asked that the words of the god be conveyed to the king. Three letters deal with messages from the god Dagan in the city of Tirqa (that is, from the god whose residence or temple was in Tirqa). One reports a dream in which Dagan grants the king victory over the hostile Benjaminites, but requests that the king send him messengers to lay all the royal affairs before him. Another instructs the king to make offerings for the spirit of the previous king. In a third Dagan tells the king through his messenger that these offerings are to be made on the fourteenth day of the following month.

More interesting is a fourth letter, in which the god Adad of the city of Kallassu requires that certain male animals be delivered by the king to him for sacrifice. The god tells the king through his intermediaries that it is he, Adad, Lord of Kallassu, who had raised the king on his own knees, had put him on the throne of his father, and had given him a residence. Let the king remember that if he does not make delivery (of the animals), 'I am the Lord of the throne, of the soil and of the city, and what I have given I can take away! If, on the contrary, he accomplishes my desire, I will give him thrones upon thrones, houses upon houses, soil upon soil, towns upon towns; and the country of the east and the west will I give him.' The royal official who sends this message to the king then adds that this is what certain persons called the *apilu* of the god have told him. He goes on to say that when formerly he lived at Mari he always conveyed to the king the messages of male and female *apilu*, and he is now continuing the same practice. Furthermore, an *apilum* of the god Adad of the city of Khalab had come with a message for the king from the god to the effect that the latter is giving him 'the country from the east to the west'.

The great majority of texts dealing with divine oracles in Mesopotamia belongs in the category of divination. The divine word was obtained by experts from various overt signs procured in various ways, e.g., from the inspection of the liver of a sacrificial animal, from eclipses, astrology, and the like. In fact, the armies of Mari had diviners for each section of troops. The texts mentioned above, however, refer to a different type of functionary. He was one who had received an oral message from a god, and he was sent by the god to deliver it personally. The message came by inspiration, and was delivered when the messenger suddenly appeared, unbidden. The name *apilum* given to such a messenger was evidently derived from a verb meaning 'to reply, answer'. This verb, like the corresponding term in the Old Testament, could be used for the revelation given by a deity to one who consulted him (1 Sam. 14. 37; 28. 6, 15). The *apilum* is the 'respondent' who makes answer for the deity.

The Mari texts appear to depict a phenomenon parallel to prophecy, and one from which it undoubtedly sprang. The Old Testament has numerous illustrations of the prophetic mediation of divine oracles (e.g., 1 Sam. 2. 27–36; 15; 2 Sam. 7; 12; 1 Kings 11. 29 ff.; 14. 1 ff.). Yet one cannot help but see a vast difference between the oracles of the God of Israel, especially as delivered by the great prophets, and those of the various gods to the king of Mari. In the Mari oracles the formal function of the *apilum* was similar to that of the prophet, but the context and range of content in the oracles were more confined. The chief concern of the various gods was to get the king to pay more attention to them, to their temples, and to their sacrifices. Threats and promises were made, and all were contingent upon whether the king gave the desired material gifts. Many of the Israelite prophets were undoubtedly concerned in equally detailed and material matters, but the greatest among them were God's charismatic instruments for the interpretation of his intention and action in the history of the time.

Maps, Texts, and Illustrations

Maps

WHA, Plates VI, XVIII; Grollenberg, Maps 11–4

Texts

(pp. 54, 62) The Story of Wenamon: *ANE*, 16–24; *ANET*, 25–9

Illustrations (The references are to Figures)

(p. 54) The Sea Peoples: Grollenberg, 187; Wright, 50–1
(p. 58) Philistine pottery: Wright, 55
(p. 58) Shiloh: Grollenberg, 175
(p. 59) The *pim* weight: *DOTT*, 13 (and pp. 229–30)
(p. 61) Megiddo: Wright, 40; *WHA*, 26
(p. 61) Megiddo ivories: *ANE*, 10, 29–31, 90; *ANEP*, 125–6, 128, 332; Wright, 41; *WHA*, 28–9
(p. 61) Beth-shan: Grollenberg, 37; Wright, 58–9; *WHA* (5th ed.), 83

CHAPTER V

THE GOLDEN AGE

THE greatest and most spectacular age of Israel was just before and after 1000 B.C. These were the days of those colorful figures, Saul, David, and Solomon, who brought the Israelite state into being and in an incredibly short time made it a nation of no small importance in the contemporary world. In the course of two generations a group of tribes, loosely knit together by a religious covenant and depending upon a spontaneous charismatic leadership to preserve their independence, became a strong and unified state. This brought material prosperity and a degree of wealth to a people who heretofore had been desperately poor.

Archaeological evidence is plentiful to indicate a 'new deal' for the farmer and prosperity for all. After the fall of Shiloh about 1050 B.C. the fortunes of Israel were at their lowest, with Philistine garrisons established in the hill country (e.g., 1 Sam. 10. 5; 13. 3) and Hebrews serving in the Philistine army (1 Sam. 14. 21). Saul's greatest service lay in his thrusting the Philistines out of the hills, while it remained for David so to reduce their power and their territory that they were never again a serious enemy. The excellent Philistine pottery with its graceful swans and attractive shapes was no longer made. In fact, the material culture of the plain became increasingly like that of the hills, showing that the center of political and economic gravity had shifted.

We are given some idea of the life of the Israelite farmer of this period by a small plaque of soft limestone which was discovered in the ruins of Gezer in 1908. It was evidently used by a schoolboy for his exercises about the time of Solomon during the 10th century, and it shows signs of repeated scraping to clear the surface for new use. The last words scratched on it were unerased; they appear to be a rhythmic enumeration of the agricultural seasons, used perhaps for memorization like the modern 'Thirty days hath September . . .' In accordance with the old Hebrew calendar the year began in mid-September. The first two months (September–November) were occupied with the olive harvest; the next two (November–January) with planting grain; the next two (January–March) with planting late crops. Flax was harvested in March–April; barley in April–May; wheat in May–June. The two months June–August were devoted, says the calendar, to the pruning of vines, though we know that this was also the time of threshing; and the final month (August–September) was given over to the harvest of summer fruit: figs, grapes, and pomegranates.

SAUL (ABOUT 1020–1000 B.C.)

The only direct light which archaeology has thrown upon the age of Saul comes from the excavation of his capital at Gibeah. Here were found the remains of his palace. The town was located three miles north of Jerusalem, on a hill overlooking the main highway north to Bethel, Shiloh, and Shechem. On this hill a town had been settled about 1200 B.C., and destroyed, probably as the result of an inter-tribal feud, a century or more later (cf. Jdg. 20). The palace-fortress built by Saul as his home upon the ruins of the earlier village, like all the better homes of the day, was at least two stories high, the family living on the second floor. A double wall surrounded the fortress, built of roughly shaped stones, with smaller stones and chips to fill the chinks. The corners were protected by strong towers, from which the defenders could hurl stones and arrows at the enemy. It would scarcely have been considered a comfortable and suitable residence by the monarchs of Egypt, Syria, or Mesopotamia, but its simplicity is just what we should expect of Saul, who was no wealthy, learned, cosmopolitan statesman, but a warrior and charismatic hero.

The contents of the fortress give further evidence of the simplicity of the life. Bronze arrowheads and sling stones, two of the commonest weapons, were found. An iron plowpoint, a whetstone, pottery, spinning wheels, rubbing stones for grinding flour, and large jars for storing grain, wine, and oil are just what we find in every Israelite home of the period. The pottery is almost entirely utilitarian, with little ornamentation. Rough, blackened cooking pots abound, as do small bowls and saucers. The finest wares were small black highly polished perfume or oil juglets, and pitchers of pink or buff color which were occasionally decorated with bands of red or brown paint around the body.

Strong as this palace-fort must have been, it was destroyed during Saul's life, possibly before the great battle of Michmash described in 1 Sam. 13–14. In any event, the palace was almost immediately rebuilt along the same lines, though the masonry was less massive and more regularly shaped and laid. What happened to it after Saul's final defeat and death on Mt. Gilboa (1 Sam. 31) we do not know. It was either again destroyed or gradually fell into ruins, out of which Judaeans a century or more later built a strong, though small, tower-fort.

DAVID (ABOUT 1000–961 B.C.)

Like Saul and the earlier judges, David was not chosen as the people's permanent leader because he had any hereditary right to the throne, but because in his person he demonstrated that he possessed special gifts, *charismata*, directly from God. He is thus the last great charismatic hero in Israel, for at the end of his reign the throne in Jerusalem became hereditary.

Israel's growth under Saul and David went hand in hand with the development of military power. David gradually gathered together his own band of professional soldiers, whose loyalties were to him alone. Later in his reign this personal army had foreign contingents in it: the Cherethites and Pelethites, probably Cretans and Philistines, but at any rate Aegean people whose ancestors had settled in Palestine about two centuries earlier. There were also six hundred warriors from the Philistine city of Gath, commanded by one Ittai (2 Sam. 15. 18). This personal army was in part responsible for the success of many of David's wars, since untrained troops from the various tribes could never have won against the powerful forces pitted against them. 2 Sam. 8 especially tells us about David's victories. First of all we know that he consolidated his home front by conquering Canaanite cities like Beth-shan and Jerusalem which had hitherto held out. Then he subdued the Philistines, the Moabites, the Ammonites, and the Edomites, imposing heavy tribute and taskwork upon them. Most remarkable of all was his subjugation of the great Aramaean (in the English Bible 'Syrian') state, the main cities of which were Damascus and Zobah. As a result, Israel became the most powerful of the small states between the Euphrates and Egypt.

There was originally a close ethnic relationship between the forefathers of the Aramaeans and the Israelites, as was pointed out in Chapter II. The Aramaeans invaded the northern part of the Fertile Crescent during the 2nd millennium, and during the time when Israel was consolidating its position in Canaan they had spread southward, forming one of their strongest states in the area of Damascus, and soon becoming the greatest traveling merchants and traders in Western Asia. Two references from the inscriptions of the kings of Assyria inform us that during the time of David's contemporary, Asshur-rabi II, the Aramaeans had conquered the territory along the upper Euphrates which had been part of the Assyrian Empire for a century. It follows that this conquest must have taken place before David's defeat and subjugation of Hadadezer, the Aramaean king. By the irony of fate, therefore, David's victory may have saved the Assyrian Empire in a period of weakness from being overrun by Aramaean hordes. At any rate, this Assyrian information certainly magnifies the greatness of David's army.

Evidence has recently been presented to indicate that David may have used the Egyptian government as a model when setting up his administration. Two lists of David's officials are preserved, presumably coming from different times in his reign (2 Sam. 8. 16–18; 20. 23–26). Of special interest are the offices of 'recorder' and 'scribe'. The functions of the 'recorder' have generally been taken to be the keeping of archives and annals, but it is not difficult to show from later passages that the position was too important for that. The original Hebrew word, however, has an exact equivalent in the title of the Egyptian Royal

Herald, who regulated the ceremonies in the palace, and was the intermediary between the king, other officers, and the people.

The office of 'scribe' again corresponds to one in Egypt. The scribe directed both interior and exterior correspondence, functioning as the royal private secretary and as secretary of state. Later copyists were apparently not sure of the name of David's scribe, since it was corrupted in transmission, but it seems to have been something like Shausha or Shisha. At any rate, it is a perfectly good Egyptian name, and it is quite possible, therefore, that David sent to Egypt for an official to fill the scribal office. It is interesting to note that the two sons of this man were Solomon's scribes and that one of them is named Elihoreph. The original Hebrew of this name is difficult to reconstruct, but with the help of the versions of the Old Testament we can say that it was probably 'Elihaph', meaning 'My God is Haph' (Apis, an Egyptian god). If this is so, then the Egyptian origin of David's scribe is virtually assured.

From the time of Solomon we find an officer in every court whose title was 'the one who is over the house', that is, over the Royal House (1 Kings 4. 6; 18. 3; 2 Kings 18. 18). This office corresponds with that of the Egyptian vizier or Prime Minister, the office held by Joseph (Gen. 41. 40). We are told in some detail what the Egyptian official's duties were. Every morning he presented himself before the king, made his report, and received his instructions. After an audience with the secretary of the treasury, he had the doors of the palace opened (and thus the various governmental offices), and the official day began. Through his hands passed all the affairs of the country. All important documents received his seal. All departments were under his orders: justice, public works, finance, armies, etc. In Israel, as in Egypt, the Prime Minister had a special robe of office, ruled in place of the king during the latter's absence or sickness, and in one place is even called the 'father' of the people (Isa. 22. 21).

'The Thirty' (2 Sam. 23. 13, 24) seems to have been an honorary military body, a legion of honor, not necessarily a fixed number, to which belonged those 'mighty men' who had distinguished themselves by feats of exceptional bravery. It has been pointed out recently that a similar organization existed in Egypt, and David may have received the idea from that source.

The 'City of David'

When David was made king over both North Israel and Judah, he was faced with the problem of establishing a neutral capital. He decided to seize Jerusalem, a city on the border between the north and the south which was still in the hands of a group of Canaanites known as Jebusites. Since it was seized by David's personal troops, it became his personal holding, and was renamed 'City of David' (2 Sam. 5. 9). We are told that he strengthened its fortifications, with the aid of Phoenician artisans built himself a palace there, reconstructed the Tabernacle, and moved the Ark of the Covenant to Jerusalem, so that from that time on Jerusalem was the religious, as well as the political, centre of the realm.

The city is located on Palestine's central limestone ridge at a point some 2,500 feet above the level of the sea where the ridge has broadened into a small plateau. Extending south from this plateau are two promontories, separated by a valley which in Roman times was called the Tyropoeon. The name of the eastern promontory was Ophel

(Mic. 4. 8 RV margin), while the name of the western in later times was Zion. To the west and south ran the Valley of Hinnom, apparently used largely as a dump and place of refuse, which in New Testament times became a synonym for Hell (Gehenna), perhaps because of the fires constantly burning there. To the east, separating Ophel from the Mount of Olives, was the Kidron Valley, in which was Jerusalem's main supply of water, the Gihon or Virgin's Fountain. The name Gihon means 'Gusher', for the spring does not produce a steady flow, but the waters apparently collect in some underground reservoir and occasionally break forth, the frequency depending on the season. To the south, below the meeting of the Kidron and Hinnom valleys, is a second spring, En-Rogel, where the great feast was held preparatory to installing Adonijah on the throne near the close of David's life (1 Kings 1). This spring is out in the open valley and could not be protected like the Gihon.

Since 1867 numerous excavations have been undertaken in Jerusalem, and a large number of remains from the ancient city have been recovered. We know that the site was occupied as early as 3000 B.C., and the actual name 'Jerusalem' occurs in Egyptian texts as early as 1900 B.C. Yet there is no sign of a 'tell' formation, that is, a mound made up of the super-imposed remains of one city upon another. The explanation is that the ancient remains were cleared away inside the city and dumped down the slopes some time during the 2nd and 1st centuries before the time of Christ. The Jewish historian Josephus tells us that a Syrian fortress built there in the early 2nd century was levelled to the ground by the Jewish patriot Simon about 140 B.C., and that the very hill on which the fortress stood was removed, the work taking three years. Thus on the slopes of Ophel, the site of the Old Testament city, there are vast quantities of debris, filled with fragments of pottery and other objects dating from the 3rd millennium to the 3rd and 2nd centuries B.C.

These remarks are necessary preparation for the disappointing statement that not a single discovery has been made in Jerusalem which can be dated with any certainty to the time of David and Solomon. We know where they lived and built, but practically everything other than the city fortifications has been destroyed. And even the complicated maze of fortifications on the hill Ophel can scarcely be disentangled and dated with any degree of certainty. The first great fortification has been traced around a section of the hill. Its two faces were made of hammer-dressed stones, sometimes of considerable size and irregularly fitted together, and smaller stones were used to fill up the chinks. The interior between the faces was filled up with stone blocks. Additional protection was provided by bastions at weak points and by towers. This system of fortification has usually been called 'Jebusite', since it is believed to have been erected by the pre-Israelite inhabitants of Jerusalem. It has been repaired in several places, and these repairs have often been called 'Davidic' and 'Solomonic', but unfortunately all these ascriptions are almost pure guesses, since there is so little evidence for the dating.

Throughout the history of the town great care was taken about the water supply in the Gihon spring. An elaborate system of tunnels in the vicinity is eloquent witness to the fact. In one early attempt to bring the water closer to those who lived inside the walls, a long aqueduct was cut along the rock scarp under the edge of the hill, running from the Gihon to the southern extremity of the city, where it emptied into a pool, called the 'old pool' (Isa. 22. 11), apparently at the mouth of the Tyropoeon Valley just inside the city walls. It was at the beginning of this aqueduct that Isaiah met Ahaz (Isa. 7. 3), if in this passage the 'upper pool' is to be identified with the Gihon, as seems probable. In another passage (8. 6) Isaiah refers to the water in this aqueduct as 'the waters of Shiloah that go softly' and uses them as a figure of God's way for Israel. This conduit was partly tunneled and partly open. Consequently it was no protection for the water supply in time of siege. For this reason Hezekiah stopped it up before 701 B.C. and built his tunnel (see Chapter VII). At that time this first aqueduct was undoubtedly old, but we can say no more about its date than we could about that of the fortifications.

SOLOMON IN ALL HIS GLORY (ABOUT 961–922 B.C.)

It was David who established the kingdom in its extent and power, but it was Solomon who added the glamor! David was a man of war, but the ideal of Solomon seems to have been that of a wealthy, worldly, cultured gentleman, and as such he busily engaged himself in the attempt to put a 'backwoods' nation on the 'civilized' map of the world. Unfortunately we do not know as much about his personality as we should like, nor do we know a great deal about the events of his career. But our sources do tell us about his building operations and commercial activities. He refortified Jerusalem, built there his palace, administrative headquarters, and Temple. In addition, he built 'store-cities' and 'the cities for his chariots and the cities for his horsemen' through the land. He was a great merchant, buying and selling horses and chariots:

> And Solomon's horses were exported from Egypt and from Cilicia (in Asia Minor where fine horses were bred).

> The merchants of the king procured them from Cilicia at the current price; and a chariot was exported from Egypt at the rate of 600 shekels of silver, and a horse (from Cilicia) at the rate of 150. And thus (at this rate) they delivered them by their agency to all the kings of the Hittites and all the kings of Aram (area of Damascus and northward) (1 Kings 10. 28–29).

We are further told that to control the Arabian and African trade Solomon, with the aid of the Phoenicians, built a fleet of ships to be based at Ezion-geber on the north-eastern arm of the Red Sea just south of Edom. This fleet made the trip southward to Ethiopia and the Arabian Yemen once every three years, bringing back gold, silver, ivory, and two kinds of monkeys (not peacocks as the English versions have it) (1 Kings 9. 26; 10. 22).

To support his elaborate court and building program the king found it necessary to institute a regular system of taxation over Israel in addition to the tribute received from the subject peoples. To this end he divided north Israel into twelve administrative districts, only roughly based on the old tribal allotments (1 Kings 4. 7 ff.). Over each he placed a district officer, one of whose main duties it was to see that his district furnished provisions for the Court one month in twelve (1 Kings 4. 22–23).

Evidence of district organization has been discovered in a number of places. At Beth-shemesh, for example, one of the main cities in the district first occupied by the tribe of Dan, the residency of the district officer, Ben-Deker, has probably been found, though it has never been completely excavated. Near by were the foundations of a large building with thick walls, high floors, and divided into three long, narrow rooms. The only conceivable purpose for such a building was to store grain and other provisions. The thick walls and high floors evidently served to keep the grain from spoiling. A similar arrangement of residency and granary has been found at Lachish in the district of Judah. Here the palace was erected on a platform with earth-filled interior, and is probably of the same type as the Millo ('Filling'?) which David built in Jerusalem (2 Sam. 5. 9). We seem to have here evidence for 'store-cities' of the type which Solomon is said to have built. The Beth-shemesh and Lachish buildings, however, are earlier than Solomon's time, and were probably erected by David. This conclusion, based on the dating of the pottery found in the ruins, may explain why nothing is said about Solomon's dividing Judah into administrative districts as he did northern Israel. It was not that Solomon was placing Judah in a favored position, but that David had already carried out the reorganization. The only detailed description of administrative districts in Judah is to be found in Josh. 15. 21–62, though in its present form this list dates from the time of Jehoshaphat in the 9th century.[1]

The great city of Megiddo in the northern plain of Esdraelon furnishes the best picture of Solomonic building thus far excavated. At first the mound seems to have been occupied only by the palace-fortress, a structure which was enclosed by a wall constructed in a way that from now on is typical of Israel, though it was probably learned from the Phoenicians. Strong piers of finely cut stone were erected every three or four feet, while in between was a filling of roughly coursed rubble. The structure was probably used largely for administrative purposes.

[1] Frank M. Cross and G. Ernest Wright, *JBL*, LXXV (1956), pp. 202–226.

Whether it was built by Solomon or David we cannot say. In any event, it was soon torn down and rebuilt as part of a large scheme to make Megiddo a major administrative stronghold and stable city (1 Kings 9. 15–19). A new wall was built around the mound, broken only by a strongly fortified gateway at the north. The Solomonic gateway recently excavated by the Israeli expedition at Hazor was built to the same plan, and the plan for the east gate of the Temple in Ezek. 40. 5–16 is very similar. Beyond the gate was a paved street, at least one branch of which led to a stable compound. Behind the stables was the paved courtyard of the district officer's residence, which was strongly built and probably had more than one story. A tower enabled him to look out over the city wall. There was another stable unit on the opposite side of the town, and in front of it a large paved courtyard with a drinking trough in the center. Various features bear witness to the help of Phoenician architects, particularly the capital used to decorate the tops of columns. It was a Phoenician adaptation of an Egyptian original, which was later borrowed by the Greeks and became their Ionic capital.

Such projects could have been built only with the aid of conscription. First, Solomon bound all the descendants of the Canaanites into state slavery (1 Kings 9. 21). In addition, he conscripted free-born Israelites themselves for the army and for the royal works projects (1 Kings 5. 13 ff.; 9. 22), and so lit the coals which immediately became a flame of revolt at the end of his reign.

The Palestinian Metal Industry

A wholly unsuspected aspect of Solomon's commercial career has been revealed through the explorations of Nelson Glueck in the valley of the Arabah, south of the

Dead Sea, and at Ezion-geber, Solomon's seaport on the Red Sea.

The soft sandstone along the eastern bank of the Arabah contains many veins of copper and iron ore. The explorations have revealed that this ore was mined during the period of Solomon and the centuries which followed with greater intensity than at any other time in history, an activity probably reflected in Deut. 8. 9. Slag heaps guide the explorer in his search. Near some of them walled enclosures have been found, within which were the ruins of the miners' huts and of the furnaces where the ore was given its preliminary smelting. The workers were almost certainly the state slaves, and the enclosures were probably walled to keep them from running away.

At Ezion-geber the excavator expected to find the ruins of Solomon's seaport (1 Kings 9. 26). No remains of the port were found, but instead there came to light a great smelting refinery, the largest ever found in the Near East. It was first built about the 10th century B.C., almost certainly, therefore, by Solomon. Ezion-geber lies in the center of a natural wind-tunnel, open to the fury of the winds and sandstorms blowing down the Arabah from the north. This must have been the reason why the site was chosen. The flues of the smelter were turned towards the north, and no bellows for forced draft would have been necessary there. The site was in other respects uninviting, and it seems probable that slave labor was employed here also.

Solomon's Temple

Solomon expended his greatest architectural energies on Jerusalem, where he built his palace, temple, and governmental headquarters. The Jebusite city on Ophel which David had conquered was far too small for Solomon's plans. He leveled a large plot to the north and included it within the city fortifications. There with the aid of Phoenician artists he began his work, and from that day to this it has been the most famous sacred area in world history.

By far the best known of his architectural wonders in Jerusalem was the Temple. Various attempts have been made to reconstruct it, but until recent years archaeological data have been lacking. Today the situation is changed, for there are many new discoveries which bear directly on our problem.

We can be fairly sure that the Temple was built after the Phoenician model, rather than the Egyptian or Mesopotamian, since 1 Kings informs us that Solomon secured the aid of Hiram, King of Tyre, for material help and technical advice. Unfortunately the temple art and architecture of Phoenicia during this period are not well known, since few excavations in contemporary city levels have been made. The small chapel of the 8th-century kings of Hattina, discovered at Tell Tainat in Syria, is the only temple contemporary with the kings of Israel (1000–600 B.C.) ever found in Syria or Palestine, but it is most important to note that its plan is very similar to that of the Temple of Solomon.

Solomon's Temple was set on a platform about 9 feet high (Ezek. 41. 8).[1] A flight of ten steps led up to the entrance, on either side of which were two free-standing columns, known as Jachin and Boaz (1 Kings 7. 21), names which were probably the first words of inscriptions on

[1] Reckoning a cubit as 18 inches for simple computation. The common cubit was actually 17½ inches, archaeological discovery has shown, while the sacred cubit which Ezekiel says was used in the Temple was one handbreadth wider or *c.* 20·4 inches. For the latest study of weights and measures, see now R. B. Y. Scott, *Biblical Archaeologist*, Vol. XXII, 2 (May 1959).

them. Their purpose or significance remain obscure, despite the many suggestions which have been made.

Inside the Temple there were three rooms. First came the vestibule or *Ulam*, then the main room of the sanctuary, the 'holy place' or *Hekal*. This room had several windows (1 Kings 6. 4) inserted in the walls below the ceiling, an arrangement which derives through the Phoenicians from the Egyptians. It was floored with cypress and lined with cedar; this feature is practically unknown in Mesopotamia, but several illustrations of it exist in the north. The roof was flat, supported by great cedar beams. The walls and the doors were decorated with palm-trees, open flowers, chains, and cherubim, carved in the cedar and inlaid (not 'overlaid' as the English versions have it) with gold leaf (1 Kings 6. 35; 2 Chr. 3. 5; Ezek. 41. 18 ff.). This carved decoration was the most Phoenician feature of all; various collections of Phoenician ivory under the strong influence of Egyptian art show us just what this sort of thing was.

Around the room was placed the sacred furniture: the golden candlesticks, the table of shewbread, and a small altar of cedar inlaid (or covered?) with gold leaf. This altar was placed directly in front of a flight of steps leading into the room beyond. This was a very familiar feature of Canaanite temples: an altar or table placed directly in front of the steps leading up to the raised 'Holy of Holies' on which was placed the statue of the god and which bore offerings of incense.

The third room was the 'Most Holy Place' or the 'Holy of Holies'. Its real name was *Debir*, 'oracle', for here was the special abode of God. This room contained no windows. What would immediately strike the eye would be the two large olivewood cherubim, which stood 15 feet high and were 'overlaid' with gold leaf. Their wings were stretched out as though for flight: the two outer wings touched the side walls, and the two inner wings touched each other in the center of the room. In all probability the Ark of the Covenant was to be found on the floor between the cherubim, beneath the outstretched wings (1 Kings 8. 6).

What were the cherubim? Why were they placed in the 'Holy of Holies', and why were they so prominent on the walls and doors? Their nature had been forgotten by the 1st century A.D. Josephus tells us that 'no one can tell what they were like'. One thing we can be sure of is that they were not the charming winged boys of Renaissance art, a conception which is traced to little beings in Graeco-Roman art. A number of scholars have thought that they were the great winged bulls which were so popular in Mesopotamia, but these are practically non-existent in the area. A process of elimination shows that the cherub can have been only one thing: a winged sphinx, that is, a winged lion with human head. This is the most popular winged being in Phoenician art.

Why was it used? Among the Megiddo ivories is a plaque which shows a Canaanite king about 1200 B.C. seated on his throne, which is a chair supported by two cherubim. Other Canaanite kings were pictured on similar thrones. Just as these monarchs were enthroned upon the cherubim, so the God of Israel is often designated 'He who thrones (or is enthroned upon) the cherubim'. In official Israelite religion it was against the law to make an image of God; so in the 'Holy of Holies' it was his invisible presence which was thought to be enthroned upon the two great hybrid beings.

The religious significance of the cherubim is rather obscure. A fragment of an ancient hymn contained the words

'And he rode upon a cherub and did fly' (2 Sam. 22. 11; Ps. 18. 10; cf. Ezek. 10. 20). Apparently, in the religion of Israel, as in other Near Eastern religions, such winged beings were thought to be assistants who aided a god in getting from place to place. We recall that in Gen. 3. 24 cherubim were placed at the east of the garden to guard the Tree of Life. This is exactly the conception which lies behind the cherubim and palm-trees carved on the walls and doors of the Temple. In Phoenician art two cherubim facing a tree is a very common motif.

On the outside of the building there was a door on both the north side and the south side, each leading to a staircase and two upper stories. In each of the three stories there was a whole series of small rooms, the ceilings of which were supported by horizontal ledges in the main wall of the Temple, so that each story is 1½ feet wider than the one below. These rooms were apparently used for storing the Temple treasure.

In the courtyard in front of the Temple stood the great altar of burnt offering and the bronze Sea. To judge from the description in Ezek. 43. 13–17, the general appearance of the altar was that of a Babylonian temple-tower (ziggurat). It was composed of three stages, each of the lower two projecting 1½ feet wider than the one above, so that a ledge was formed around each stage. The topmost stage was the hearth for burnt offerings. It was called *harel*, meaning probably 'mountain of God', evidently a popular etymology of an Akkadian term which could refer either to the underworld or to the cosmic mountain on which the gods were thought to live. A flight of steps on the east led up to the altar's hearth.

The bronze Sea was a great bowl, 15 feet in diameter and 7½ feet high. It was made of cast bronze, about 3 inches thick, and its brim was ornamented (1 Kings 7. 23 ff.). It rested on the backs of twelve oxen arranged in threes, each triad facing one of the points of the compass. Such a bronze bowl would weigh between 25 and 30 tons, with which may be compared the bell of St. Paul's in London (17½ tons). The Sea and the pillars were cast in the clay beds of the Jordan Valley, not far from the place where the River Jabbok flows into the Jordan (1 Kings 7. 13 ff., 46).

A later record tells us that the Sea was for the special use of the priests as a place where they could wash (2 Chr. 4. 6). But why was it called 'Sea'? The Jewish historian Josephus said it was so named because of its size. In all probability, however, it had a symbolic meaning. The sea played an important part in Canaanite and Babylonian mythology. To the Babylonians it was the ultimate source of all life and fertility, and it was also the abode of the Canaanite Leviathan, the dragon of chaos. Solomon's bronze Sea, therefore, like the cherubim and the columns, was used because it had had a long history in the theology of Canaan. Its ultimate fate, however, was assured. There was too much valuable bronze in it. King Ahaz took the oxen from under it to pay tribute to the Assyrian king in 734 B.C., and the Babylonians broke up the bowl and carried the fragments to Babylon after the capture of Jerusalem in 587 B.C. (2 Kings 16. 17; 25. 13).

The Theological Meaning of the Temple

In the ancient polytheistic world kingship and temple were the two institutions which bound the divine and human worlds together. In Egypt the king was the incarnate son of the Sun-god. In Mesopotamia he was the selected representative of the gods to rule the earthly society, and could be thought of as the gods' adopted 'son'.

In Israel the king was conceived in a similar way, and could be called in this sense God's son (2 Sam. 7. 14; Ps. 2. 7).

In Babylon one of the chief religious functions of the king was to preside over the annual New Year's celebration. Central in this celebration was a cult drama in which the creation battle was refought and rewon, and as a result the order of nature was believed to have been established for the ensuing year. The king took the part of the king of the gods in the drama, on the principle of sympathetic magic, of like making like. By imitative action the king could identify himself with a god and thus accomplish what the god had accomplished, for to the polytheistic mind what is like is in some measure identical with what is. In another ceremony the king identified himself with the god of rain and vegetation, while a priestess became the goddess of fertility, and their union represented the union of the creative powers of the spring. Thus in the festival rites in the temple the pagan king created anew the orderly world in the battle against chaos, and he secured the fertility and revival of nature in spring and fall.

Some scholars believe that a New Year's festival comparable to that in Babylon existed in Israel and was celebrated by the Israelite king in the Solomonic Temple. In the festival as conducted by the Davidic dynasty the enemies of God were not believed to be the dragons of chaos but historical powers who refuse God's rule. In the rites their defeat was celebrated as though it had already taken place or was about to do so. Other scholars feel very strongly that the supposed parallel between the Babylonian and Israelite festivals in the Temple does not really exist. While there must have been services in the Temple which employed a number of the Psalms to celebrate God's defeat of earthly enemies and the role of the Davidic king as God's agent in the defeat (Pss. 2; 110), sympathetic magic played little part in the ceremonies. The work was or would be God's doing.

The importance of king and temple in pagan life is clear. The stability of nature and of society was believed to be dependent on what went on in the temple services. The temple was indeed 'none other than the house of God . . . the gate of heaven' (Gen. 28. 17), and 'the foundation-platform of heaven and earth' (the name given the temple-tower of Babylon). Although in Israel the Sinai covenant had established a relationship between people and deity which was prior to kingship and the temple, yet the term 'house of God' was continued as the Temple's name, as was the term 'palace' (*hekal*). The ancient Near East seems not to have possessed a special term like our 'temple' for a religious edifice. It was simply the house or palace in which the divine lord resided together with his divine and human servants. The human servants, the priests, had charge of the building and the property belonging to it, for their real task was to make provision for the god's needs. This was the significance of the daily cult. The sacrifices, offerings, and libations were the god's needed food and drink.

In Israel, however, there were limits to the anthropomorphic conception of deity. The great Lord had no physical needs which man could supply (cf. Ps. 50. 12–13). The whole sacrificial system, while in outward form it resembled the systems of polytheism, had a different setting and purpose. It was a form which God accepted for worship, praise, thanksgiving, communion, and especially for atonement of sin, provided that the sins were not of the presumptuous, high-handed, rebellious type which indicated a hardened, disloyal heart. For such sins sacramentalism was of no avail.

How could a cosmic god, such as the sky, the storm, the sun, or the moon, be conceived as living in an earthly house? This is a problem to our logical minds, and it was to some in Israel, as we shall see, but it was not so to the polytheist. The ancient temple was filled with cosmic symbolism, so that it was conceived to be a microcosm, a replica in miniature, of the cosmic world in which the deity lived. Since like is like, the temple which is like the universe is in a measure that universe, and the limitless deity thus could inhabit it. His presence was indicated by his statue placed in the building. Yet the statue did not confine him: he was numinously present in it, but he was still the cosmic power, to be met in his temple and yet to be met also in the experience of power in nature.

The Solomonic Temple was erected in all probability with no more conscious awareness of this problem than existed in polytheism. It was simply the 'house of Yahweh', and his presence was believed to be invisibly enthroned in the darkness over the cherubim in the Holy of Holies. Yet in the course of time the problem was seen and evidently discussed. In the Deuteronomic prayer attributed to Solomon at the dedication of the Temple there is a denial of the whole polytheistic notion that God can dwell like a human being on earth. His dwelling is in heaven. The Temple is simply the bearer of his Name and a house of prayer, or rather the focus of religious attention to which prayer is directed (1 Kings 8. 27–30).

How the priests, who cared for the Temple and its services, interpreted its meaning is not entirely clear. Central to priestly theology was the conception of God's presence in the midst of his people. This presence was the people's blessing and security, and to Ezekiel the vision of God's departure from the Temple was the sign of his determination to destroy it (Ezek. 10–11). Yet that the priests were conscious of the problem is indicated by their terminology. The common term used for human sitting or dwelling on earth was *yashabh*. The priests were careful not to use this term to indicate God's presence in the Temple, but instead used the term *shakan*, an old nomadic word meaning 'to tent' or 'to tabernacle'. By the use of a technical terminology they suggest that while God's 'dwelling' is in heaven, the mystery of his presence is nevertheless known on earth, for he 'tabernacles' in the midst of his people.

Maps, Texts, and Illustrations

Maps

WHA, Plates VIIA, XVIIA, XVIII; Grollenberg, Maps 15–6, 24A, B

Texts

(p. 67) Gezer Calendar: *ANE*, 209; *ANET*, 320; *DOTT*, 201–3

(p. 85) Program for the Babylonian New Year Festival: *ANET*, 331–4

Illustrations (The references are to Figures)

(p. 67 Gezer Calendar: *ANE*, 65; *ANEP*, 272; *DOTT*, 11; Wright, 130

(p. 67) Gibeah: Wright, 74–5

(p. 68) Weapons and utensils: *ANEP*, 141; Wright, 57

(p. 72) Jerusalem: Grollenberg 191–2; *WHA* (5th ed.), 82

(p. 77) Solomonic Megiddo: *ANE*, 181, 183; *ANEP*, 721, 741–2; Grollenberg, 209–10; Wiseman, 47; Wright, 82–7

(p. 78) Solomonic Hazor: *ANE*, 174
(p. 79) Furnace in Arabah: Wright, 88
(p. 79) Refinery at Ezion-geber: Wright, 89, 111
(p. 80) Temple at Tell Tainat: *ANE*, 185; *ANEP*, 739; Grollenberg, 198; Wright, 91
(p. 80) Reconstruction of Solomon's Temple: Wright, 92; *WHA*, 31
(p. 81) Phoenician ivory: Grollenberg, 211–17; Wright, 90
(p. 83) Altar of burnt offering: Wright, 93; *WHA* (5th ed.), 32
(p. 83) Bronze Sea: Wright, 94

CHAPTER VI

DIVISION AND DOWNFALL

THE golden age of the great kings did not survive the 10th century. Owing to the policies of Solomon, the kingdom split apart. North Israel retained the name 'Israel' for itself and chose as its king Jeroboam, who had once been the Solomonic officer in charge of the northern compulsory labor battalions. The southern kingdom, calling itself 'Judah', retained the Davidic dynasty. The boundary between the two was the northern border of the old tribal area of Benjamin, 10 miles north of Jerusalem. The large empire established by David was now no more. The Aramaean state centering in Damascus had broken away and was independent. The kingdom of Ammon across the Jordan, with capital at the modern Amman, had either attained its independence or was shortly to do so, to judge from the mention of an independent king of that territory by the Assyrian monarch Shalmaneser III in 853 B.C. (cf. also 2 Chr. 20. 1). Israel also soon lost its control of Moab to the east of the Dead Sea, and seems not to have reconquered it before 875 B.C., while the land of Bashan, east of the Sea of Galilee, was shortly seized by Damascus. Edom for a time may have gained its independence from Judah (cf. 1 Kings 11. 14–22), though during the first half of the 9th century it was again under the firm control of the Jerusalem court (cf. 1 Kings 22. 47).

Despite political instability in the north, and constant

bickering between north and south, when external factors allowed, there seems to have been a great deal of prosperity among the people of the land. In certain places at least our excavated evidence indicates a gradual increase in the population and a general improvement in the standard of living. It is especially interesting to see in those places where blocks of Israelite houses have been well preserved that on the whole the home of a Hebrew in Canaan was now somewhat better than that of a Canaanite peasant of the 14th or 13th century during the period of greatest decadence in Canaanite culture.

The material culture of Palestine has now become exceedingly uniform, and the remnants of the Canaanite and Philistine cultures in the plain areas have largely disappeared under the economic domination of the people in the hills. In addition, we now enter a period when for over 300 years the customs of the people are so stable that it is difficult for archaeologists to fix clear cultural phases. Even pottery is difficult to date precisely. We can now date a representative collection of dishes, pots, and jars to the 9th–8th or to the 8th–7th centuries, but that is usually as close as we can come with any degree of certainty. This stability of culture reflects a certain stability of life and thought in spite of the many political upheavals.

Archaeology and Politics

Jeroboam, we are told, 'built' Shechem as his new capital in North Israel (1 Kings 12. 25). As it had been the chief city of the area for at least a thousand years, the phrase 'built Shechem' presumably refers to the fortification of the city, and some of Jeroboam's work has probably been discovered. He evidently repaired the older city wall, and one fragment of this repair had been unearthed. At the north-west the old city gate of Canaanite times was re-used, and the same is true of the Canaanite East Gate, where the Drew–McCormick Expedition in 1956 found evidence of Jeroboam's very insubstantial rebuilding.

We are told that since Jerusalem had become the religious capital of all Israel, Jeroboam became worried lest this should prove a divisive factor and endanger his throne. Consequently he made two golden calves (or rather bulls) and set them up in the two cities which had been hallowed by previous tradition, Dan and Bethel. At these two places he established the religious services and told his people to worship there instead of at Jerusalem (1 Kings 12. 26 ff.).

How are these bulls to be interpreted? Were they supposed to be idols, representing the God of Israel? The later religious leaders seem to have interpreted them in this way, or in any event to have believed that they led the people into idolatry. It is improbable, however, that Jeroboam intended to turn away from the God of Israel. Neighboring peoples were accustomed to represent their gods as standing on the backs of animals or else seated on thrones borne by animals. The second is the conception borrowed by Solomon for his Temple in Jerusalem. The first was probably in the mind of Jeroboam; to him the golden bull may have been the pedestal on which the invisible Lord was thought to stand. It is easy to see, however, that the people would believe they were worshipping what they could see, the bull itself, especially as El and Baal were frequently likened to bulls in Canaanite religion.

The first great disaster since the reign of Saul descended upon the two kingdoms about 918 B.C. Our books of Kings give us scant information about it:

> And it came to pass in the fifth year of king Rehoboam that Shishak king of Egypt came up against Jerusalem. And he took away the treasures of the house (Temple) of the Lord, and the treasures of the king's house. . . . And he took away all the shields of gold which Solomon had made (1 Kings 14. 25–26).

This king of Egypt thought more highly of his campaign, however, and on the walls of the great temple of Karnak in upper Egypt he had his artists carve a picture of himself smiting the Asiatics in the presence of the god Amon, who with a goddess is depicted as presenting to him ten lines of captives. Each captive symbolized a town or locality, the name of which was inscribed below. From these names we can gather the extent of his campaign. The biblical account implies that only Judah was affected, but all of Palestine apparently suffered, for the list includes cities in the Esdraelon, Transjordan, the hill country of Israel, and even Edom. Shishak was attempting to restore the great Egyptian empire of bygone days, and since his army was composed of wild African troops from Libya and Nubia (he himself was a Libyan), the devastation can readily be imagined (cf. 2 Chr. 12. 2 ff.).

The excavations have further supported the extent and severity of the conquest. A fragment of a monumental stone or *stele* set up by the king at Megiddo has been found at the site. A number of towns are known or suspected to have been at least partially destroyed, among them Debir, Tell Jemmeh (Jorda?) south of Gaza, and even Solomon's great refinery at Ezion-geber. Mammoth fortifications unearthed at Sharuhen (modern Tell el-Far'ah), south-east of Gaza, if correctly ascribed to Shishak, show that the king was making no mere raid but an occupation in force, employing thousands of laborers. The conquest was short-lived, however. Shishak died soon after consolidating his conquest, and his successors were not as energetic or able (2 Chr. 14. 9 ff.).

The Dynasty of Omri (about 876–842 B.C.)[1]

The story of how Omri became king is told in 1 Kings 16. 8 ff. His dynasty was the most notorious Israel ever had, thanks to his son Ahab's marriage to Jezebel, the daughter of Itto-baal (Ethbaal), a priest of Astarte in Tyre, who had seized the Phoenician throne by murdering his predecessor. Seven verses (1 Kings 16. 21–28) give us the sole biblical information about Omri himself, but these verses when combined with archaeological information indicate that he was a king of considerable ability. The Assyrians on many occasions referred to Israel as 'the land of Omri' or 'the house of Omri' long after revolution had destroyed all remnants of the dynasty.

Our most direct evidence, however, comes from the excavations of Samaria. Shechem, the natural capital of North Israel, was not a place which could easily be defended. Consequently Omri's immediate predecessors had used Tirzah as their capital. Tirzah was probably located at the modern Tell el-Far'ah, a large mound about 7 miles north-east of Shechem. An expedition under Father de Vaux began to excavate it in 1947, and found that it was first established in the 4th millennium, was a great city throughout the Bronze Age, and was destroyed in the early 9th as well as in the 8th century B.C. The city's history conforms to that of Tirzah, but not enough information is available to make the identification certain.

[1] The chronology of the Divided Monarchy which is followed here is for the most part that of W. F. Albright, *BASOR*, No. 100 (December 1945), pp. 16–22. Many of the dates are only approximate.

Omri, aligning his kingdom with Phoenicia, chose a new capital, the hill of Samaria, some 7 miles north-west of Shechem on the road to Esdraelon, Galilee, and Phoenicia. The first Palestinian archaeologist, Edward Robinson, said of it: 'It would be difficult to find, in all Palestine, a situation of equal strength, fertility, and beauty combined. In all these particulars it has greatly the advantage over Jerusalem.'[1]

The city of Samaria is very difficult to excavate, because it was intensively occupied both before and after the time of Jesus, and builders in Hellenistic and Roman times erected such great structures on bed rock that the Israelite strata were disturbed and in many places removed entirely. Actual remains of Israelite days are therefore comparatively few, and in a chaotic ruined state. Buildings and walls can be traced to some extent, however, and even where the walls have disappeared, it is possible to trace where they once were, because the architects not only laid them on bed rock, but leveled the rock, even cutting trenches in it, before the foundations were laid.

Five phrases of Israelite building have been distinguished, all dating between about 875 B.C., when the city was first established by Omri, and 721 B.C., when it was destroyed by the Assyrians. Period I can be ascribed to both Omri and Ahab: that is, Omri began the construction, but owing to the short time in which he reigned, we must assume that his work was completed by his son Ahab. The fortifications consisted of a wall around the summit of the mound, which enclosed a large palace and courtyard. This was in turn enclosed by two more walls, the first slightly lower on a terrace and the other around the base of the hill. The stone masonry is of such superb

[1] *Biblical Researches in Palestine*, II (1841), p. 307.

workmanship that nothing has ever been found in Palestine that surpasses it. The city gate on the summit was evidently on the east, probably approached by a monumental forecourt in which there were pilasters with 'proto-Ionic' capitals.

In the ruins of the city were many pieces of ivory which had once been used as inlays to decorate boxes and fine furniture. Amos refers to those who lie upon beds of ivory (Amos 6. 4; cf. 3. 15), and the remains of one such bed, decorated with ivory inlay, have actually been found at the site of Arslan Tash in northern Syria, one of the pieces bearing the name of Hazael, King of Damascus in the time of Jehu of Israel (about 842–815 B.C.). From 1 Kings 22. 39 we learn that Ahab built an 'ivory house', that is a building decorated on the interior with ivory, and it may be that the excavators found the ruins of this building, since a large number of the ivory pieces were found in and around the foundations of one building. The workmanship of the ivories was undoubtedly Phoenician and Damascene, and we would assume that they were imported or made by imported artists.

The reign of Ahab was marked by intermittent war with Damascus, but in 854–853 Ahab joined in a strong coalition with Damascus and a number of other states, including Ammon and perhaps Egypt, against Shalmaneser III of Assyria. Battle was joined in 853 B.C. at Qarqar on the River Orontes, north of Damascus. For some reason this battle is unmentioned in the Bible, and we know of it only from the reports of Shalmaneser. The latter tells us that the three main kings of the opposition were Hadadezer of Damascus, with 1,200 chariots, 1,200 cavalrymen, and 20,000 infantry; Irhuleni of Hamath with 700 chariots, 700 cavalrymen, and 10,000 infantry; and 'Ahab the

Israelite' with 2,000 chariots and 10,000 infantry. The horse and chariot as a weapon of war had been introduced into Israel by David and Solomon (2 Sam. 8. 4; 1 Kings 10. 26), and Ahab now possessed more of them than his neighbors, though as yet Israel made no use of cavalry. Shalmaneser claimed a great victory at Qarqar. In one inscription he claims to have killed 14,000 soldiers of the combined army, spanning the Orontes on the corpses 'before there was a bridge'. In another place he claims the number was 20,500, and in still another the figure is 25,000. Scholars believe the monarch's claim was exaggerated. Even if he did win the day, he must have suffered very heavy losses himself, for he did not follow up the victory. Indeed, time after time in the years which followed he returned to Syria, claimed victory, but did not take Damascus or march into Palestine.

Within three years after Qarqar Ahab was again fighting the armies of Damascus in the attempt to win back northern Transjordan, but he lost his life in the battle. After his death, during the reign of his son Joram (about 849–842 B.C.), King Mesha of Moab successfully rebelled (2 Kings 1. 1; 3. 4 ff.). Mesha commemorated this event by erecting what is now known as the 'Moabite Stone'. This monument was discovered at the Moabite capital, Dibon, in 1868. On it Mesha tells us that Omri of Israel had humbled Moab for many years because the Moabite god 'Chemosh was angry at his land. And his son followed him and he also said, "I will humble Moab." In my time he spoke (thus), but I have triumphed over him and over his house, while Israel hath perished for ever!'[1]

[1] *ANET*, p. 320.

THE DYNASTY OF JEHU (ABOUT 842–745 B.C.)

That Jehu was on the throne of Israel by 841 B.C. is indicated by Assyrian records, which claim that he paid tribute to Shalmaneser at that time. The Assyrian king on his 'Black Obelisk' presents the first pictures of Israelites that we know. His artist represents Jehu kissing the ground before Shalmaneser. Behind him is a line of Israelites, bearing a variety of tribute. Above the pictures are the following words: 'The tribute of Jehu, son of Omri; I received from him silver, gold, a golden *saplu*-bowl, a golden vase with pointed bottom, golden tumblers, golden buckets, tin, a staff for a king, (and) wooden *purukhtu*.'[1]

The Jehu revolt broke the alliances which the Omri dynasty had made with Phoenicia and Judah, so that Israel was left isolated. The kingdom did not again join with Damascus in attempting to repel Shalmaneser. After 837 B.C. Damascus was not again troubled by Assyria until 805 B.C., when her kingdom was devastated and forced to pay heavy tribute to Shalmaneser's successor. Meanwhile Hazael King of Damascus, to whom the Assyrians allude as a 'son of nobody' (i.e., a commoner; cf. 2 Kings 8. 7–15), was able to deal blow after blow to Israel and also to Judah, until by about 810 B.C. Judah had paid heavy tribute to him and Israel was in such a weakened condition that she could scarcely defend herself (2 Kings 12. 17–13. 23). It was probably in this period that the Solomonic city of Megiddo was destroyed. Some rebuilding in Megiddo had been necessary after the Shishak invasion (*c.* 918 B.C.), including a new city-gate. Yet the main structure of the city, including stables and governor's palace, continued in use. Now, however, they were destroyed, presumably by

[1] *ANET*, p. 281.

Hazael, and the new city of Stratum III was constructed on an entirely new plan.

At Samaria the remains are more difficult to date. Period II at the Israelite capital is marked by an elaborate new fortification which replaced the Omri–Ahab inner wall around the summit of the mound. On the north, west, and part of the south side of the mound a 'casemate' wall was built: that is, there were two parallel walls joined together by cross walls. The style of the construction is the same as that of the preceding Omri–Ahab Period I. The work was so beautifully and strongly done that it was kept in repair and used for centuries, not being replaced until about 150 B.C. by the 'Hellenistic Fort Wall', which was erected as a defense against the Maccabees. Within the city there is evidence for a destruction of this building phase, so that Period III is marked by a great deal of reconstruction, including, it would appear, the rebuilding of the royal palace. Yet the pottery fragments suggest to the excavators that Periods I and II are very close together in time, and that Period III is not to be dated very long after them. On the other hand, the last two Israelite periods at Samaria (IV, and V–VI) appear separated by a considerable interval from the first three, and probably represent rebuilding and repair in the last decades before the city's destruction by the Assyrians in 721 B.C. If the excavators are correct in seeing evidence of destruction for Period II, it is not unlikely that we should look to Hazael of Damascus for its cause. If so, then Jehu himself may have erected the casemate wall as an added protection for his capital, though at the moment we cannot be sure.[1]

[1] The chronology of the Samaria ruins is not that of the excavators, but my own. For technical details, see G. Ernest Wright, 'Israelite Samaria and Iron Age Chronology', *BASOR* 155 (October 1959), pp. 13–29.

In any event it was during the reigns of Joash and Jeroboam II (between 801 and 746 B.C.) that Israel reached the height of her power and prosperity. Period III at Samaria, with its rebuilding of the royal palace, is probably to be dated in this time. The Assyrian kings were occupied at home and left the west virtually undisturbed. Jeroboam II was thus able to conquer Damascus and to restore the old Davidic border on the north in eastern Syria (2 Kings 14. 25, 28).

It is to this period that a group of sixty-three potsherds from Samaria, with ink inscriptions on them, is to be assigned. They were discovered in 1910 in the ruins of a building west of the royal palace. The contents of the documents at first sight appear most uninteresting. Typical of them are the following: No. 1: 'In the tenth year. To Shamariah from Beeryam, a jar of old wine. Pega (son of) Elisha, 2; Uzza (son of) . . ., 1; Eliba, 1; Baala (son of) Elisha, 1; Jedaiah, 1'; No. 55: 'In the tenth year. (From the) vineyard of Yehau-eli. A jar of fine oil,'[1] These *ostraca* prove to be administrative dockets which record shipments of wine and oil to Samaria from various towns and districts of the tribal area of western Manasseh. Whether the shipments were tax payments of the government or produce from crown lands is debated. Nevertheless, it is certain that they belong in some way to the royal fiscal organization.

The dates on the documents are the 9th, 10th, and 15th years of an unnamed king, and the last one, No. 63, seems to have the 17th year written on it. This was the way events were dated in Palestine. Of the two kings of this period only Jeroboam II (about 786–746 B.C.) reigned seventeen or more years. Hence the *ostraca* are presumably

[1] *ANET*, p. 321.

to be dated about 778, 777, 772, and 770 B.C. Their primary importance lies in the fact that they list a number of villages and districts in an area about which we have little information in ancient times. Some of the names still survive in those of modern villages, whereas some of the districts correspond to the names of Manasseh's descendants as preserved in Num. 26. 29–33 and 1 Chr. 7. 14–19: e.g., Abiezer, Hoglah, Helek, Noah, Shechem, and Shemida. This proves what scholars have previously suspected, that the sons and daughters of Manasseh in the biblical lists are actually clans, many of which with the aid of the *ostraca* can now be located on the map.

Furthermore, the proper names on the documents are good biblical names, though a surprising number of them contain the element *baal* ('lord'). In biblical times it was customary for parents to name their children with a sentence, which often began or ended with the name or title of a god: thus Jonathan means 'Yahweh has given', Obadiah 'servant of Yahweh', etc. In early Israel *baal* as a title for Yahweh had been borrowed from Canaan along with other divine epithets, but the prophetic reaction against the use of *baal* was very strong because of the danger of confusing the title with that of the great Canaanite storm-god, for whom it was now used almost exclusively as a proper name (cf. Hos. 2. 16–17). Thus far no instances of *baal*-names are known from Judah during the 8th and 7th centuries. Yet the fact that they are still so frequent in the Samaria *ostraca* indicates that the revolt of Jehu, while re-establishing Yahweh as the god of the nation, had not had a deep theological impact on some of the people.

Finally, the numbers on the documents indicate that Israel, like other peoples of the day, had a system for writing numbers without using their names. A single vertical stroke was 1, two verticals was 2, a vertical with a horizontal bar meeting the top at the left was 5, and two slanting strokes which formed a triangle with open bottom was 10. The signs for 10 and 5, when written together, stood for 15.

In Judah during the early part of the 8th century the great king was Uzziah, also known as Azariah (about 783–742 B.C.). One of Uzziah's deeds which can be verified archaeologically is the statement that he built Elath and restored it to Judah (2 Kings 14. 22). The town of Elath is the same as Ezion-geber, where Solomon built his great copper refinery. It appears to have been destroyed when Edom gained her independence from Judah during the forties of the 9th century. Uzziah's father had re-subjugated Edom, and now Uzziah himself rebuilt the refinery. Not only did the excavator, Nelson Glueck, discover the remains of Uzziah's city, but in it was a beautifully designed seal, in a copper casing, bearing the inscription *lytm* ('belonging to Jotham') above the figure of a horned ram. While we cannot be sure, the seal's owner may have been Uzziah's son of that name, who became regent during his father's leprosy. In any event, it is a good Judaean name. Elath and Edom were lost by Judah early in the reign of Jotham's son Ahaz, that is, about 734 B.C. (2 Kings 16. 6 RSV).

The Fall of Israel

In 745–744 a new Assyrian king came to the throne in Nineveh after a revolt; he was Tiglath-pileser III (*c.* 745–727 B.C.). Within the first years of his reign he was hard at work in Syria with a great army, beginning the complete subjugation of the Syro-Palestinian coastland. Soon northern Syria was firmly in his hands, and the eastern part of it was formed into an Assyrian province, ruled by an Assyrian governor from Arpad (cf. 2 Kings 18. 34; 19. 13).

Jeroboam II of Israel, its last strong king, died just before these events (about 746 B.C.). From then on, evidently because of Assyrian pressure, we hear of civil war and frequent revolts. Uzziah was still king in Jerusalem, though he was a leper and confined to separate quarters. In Syria Tiglath-pileser was confronted with a coalition, headed by one Azriau (Azariah) of Yauda (Judah). The identification with Uzziah has seemed so improbable that many scholars have felt that there must have been a Judah in the north with a king who bore the name of the Hebrew God Yahweh. But we have no other information about such a kingdom and little room for it among the known city-states of Syria. The view that it was the southern Judah under Uzziah which was involved has therefore recently been taken up again. This would mean that in the years 744–742 Uzziah of Judah was one of the outstanding personalities of Western Asia and the focus for the opposition to Assyria. He died about 742 B.C., before Assyrian retribution could catch him. At any rate his name suddenly disappeared from the Assyrian records.

In 738 B.C. we hear that Menahem of Israel paid tribute to 'Pul' (a personal name of Tiglath-pileser). Having received a thousand talents of silver, Pul confirmed Menahem's hold on the royal power (2 Kings 15. 19). Tiglath-pileser in one of his inscriptions corroborates the Biblical statement. He says that he 'overwhelmed' Menahem so that the latter 'fled like a bird, alone' and bowed at his feet. The Assyrian returned Menahem to his throne, and imposed on him a tribute of 'gold, silver, linen garments, with multicolored trimmings . . .'

The crucial years, however, were those between 735 and

732 B.C. Ahaz of Judah refused to join in a coalition of Damascus and Israel against Assyria, and when they turned to attack him he appealed to Tiglath-pileser for help (2 Kings 16. 7). Ahaz sent a large 'present' to the Assyrian; the latter raided Palestine, captured Galilee from Israel, took many into captivity (2 Kings 15. 29), besieged Damascus, carried away its king, and carried away captives (2 Kings 16. 9). Tiglath-pileser confirms this account and adds several details. He began by taking the Philistine plain as far south as Gaza, all of Naphtali (Galilee), and Transjordan from Israel, and finally disposed of Damascus. He further says that the territory taken from Israel was united with Assyria, and 'officers of mine I installed as governors upon them'. This means that as a result of this campaign Israel was left as a small territory in the hill country west of Jordan, while Galilee became an Assyrian province. Furthermore, we know that Tiglath-pileser had introduced a new policy of deporting the leading citizens from conquered territories, settling them elsewhere, while importing new groups into the depleted areas. This is the first known case of large-scale reshuffling of populations in order to keep them submissive.

In all probability it was at this time that the city of Megiddo (Stratum III) was destroyed by Tiglath-pileser and then rebuilt as the administrative capital of the Assyrian province of Galilee. In the new city of Stratum II the old Solomonic city wall was no longer used. The site was dominated by a tremendous palace-fort on the eastern side of the mound, part of it resting on the old city wall. This was probably the headquarters of the new Assyrian commandant and of the troops stationed there to preserve order.

The city of Hazor in Galilee was also destroyed at this

time (2 Kings 15. 29), and the citadel has been identified by the recent Israeli expedition. A wine jar found amid the debris was inscribed *lpqh*, 'belonging to Pekah'. As this was the name of the King of Israel at the time, the jar could well have belonged to the royal adminstration.

As aftermath to the severe setback given Israel in 733 B.C. Pekah was killed in a revolt and Hoshea became king (2 Kings 15. 30). Tiglath-pileser's view was that vassal kings were enthroned only on his authority: 'They overthrew their king Pekah and I placed Hoshea as king over them.' Ahaz in Judah remained a loyal and obedient vassal, and Tiglath-pileser lists his name among the tribute-paying western kings. Ahaz lost a number of border towns to the Philistine cities (2 Chr. 28. 18), and Edom was able to secure its independence, never again to come under Judaean control. The smelter at Elath was destroyed by fire, and a new Edomite industrial village was built over the ruins.

Hoshea, Israel's last king, became the vassal of Tiglath-pileser's successor, Shalmaneser V (727–722 B.C.), but withheld tribute (2 Kings 17. 3–4). Shalmaneser attacked him in 724 B.C., took him prisoner, and besieged Samaria. In 722 Shalmaneser died, and Sargon II, his successor, claimed the honor of victory at the very end of 722 or early in 721 B.C. Sargon repeatedly boasted of this victory in his inscriptions. In one of them he wrote: 'I besieged and conquered Samaria, led away as booty 27,290 inhabitants of it. I formed from among them a contingent of 50 chariots [for the royal corps] and made the remaining (inhabitants) assume their (social) positions. I installed over them an officer of mine and imposed upon them the tribute of the former king.'[1]

[1] *ANET*, pp. 284–285.

Thus the curtain was drawn over an independent Israel. Within a short time also part of the Philistine plain along the coast was reorganized into an Assyrian province, so that Judah alone was left with a semblance of independence.

Maps, Texts, and Illustrations

Maps

WHA, Plates VIIB, XVIII; Grollenberg, Maps 17–8

Texts

(p. 93) Shishak's inscription: *ANE*, 187; *ANET*, 263–4

(p. 96) Shalmaneser's account of the battle of Qarqar: *ANE*, 189–91; *ANET*, 278–9; *DOTT*, 47

(p. 97) The Moabite Stone: *ANE*, 209–10; *ANET*, 320–1; *DOTT*, 195–8

(p. 98) The Black Obelisk of Shalmaneser: *ANET*, 281; *DOTT*, 48

(p. 100) The Samaria *ostraca*: *ANE*, 211; *ANET*, 321; *DOTT*, 204–8

(p. 102) Tiglath-pileser and Azriau of Yauda: *ANET*, 282–3; *DOTT*, 54–5

(p. 104) Tiglath-pileser and the Damascus–Israel coalition: *ANE*, 194; *ANET*, 283–4; *DOTT*, 55

(p. 105) Sargon and the Fall of Samaria: *ANE*, 195–6; *ANET*, 284–5; *DOTT*, 59–63

Illustrations (The references are to Figures)

(p. 92) Hadad on the back of a bull: *ANE*, 140; *ANEP*, 500–1; Grollenberg, 219, 257; Wright, 97

(p. 93) Shishak's inscription: *ANE*, 94

(p. 94) Excavations at Tell el-Far'ah: Grollenberg, 62–9

(p. 95) Samaria: *ANE*, 177; *ANEP*, 718; Grollenberg, 224–5, 227; Wright, 100–5; *WHA* (5th ed.), 34–5

(Contemporary Hazor, exhibiting similar architecture; *ANE*, 174)

(p. 96) Ivories from Samaria: *ANEP*, 129–30; Wright, 103

(p. 97) The Moabite Stone: *ANE*, 74; *ANEP*, 274; *DOTT*, 10; Grollenberg, 229; Wiseman, 48; Wright, 106; *WHA*, 32; (5th ed.), 33

(p. 98) The Black Obelisk of Shalmaneser: *ANE*, 100; *ANEP*, 351–5; *DOTT*, 3; Grollenberg, 247; Wiseman, 3, 50–1; Wright, 107–8; *WHA*, 49; (5th ed.), 53

(p. 100) The Samaria *ostraca:* Grollenberg, 220

(p. 102) The Jotham Seal: *DOTT*, 13 (and pp. 224–5); Wright, 110c

CHAPTER VII

THE LAST DAYS OF JUDAH

OVER a century and a quarter of semi-independent life remained to Judah after the destruction of Samaria in 721 B.C. Fragmentary remains at Samaria indicate its reoccupation; among them is said to be an alien pottery which may well have been brought to the city by the displaced people from other parts of the Near East whom the Assyrians settled there (2 Kings 17. 24). King Hezekiah (*c.* 715–687 B.C.) promptly moved to reunite north and south religiously, as a preparation for political reunion (2 Chr. 29–31). He was thus reasserting the claims of the Davidic dynasty for a united Palestine. Failing in his political objective, he became the head of a coalition of small states, and with the promise of Egyptian and Babylonian backing he revolted against Sennacherib, when the latter succeeded Sargon in 705 B.C. (2 Kings 18–20). Sennacherib retaliated in 701 B.C., and from him we get a fuller report of the events.

According to Sennacherib's annals, Hezekiah had intervened in Philistine affairs in order to strengthen local rebels, even imprisoning in Jerusalem Padi, King of Ekron, 'unlawfully, as though he were an enemy'. Sennacherib further speaks of 'the overbearing and proud Hezekiah', who became afraid and called on the Ethiopian King of Egypt for aid. The latter responded with bowmen, chariotry, and cavalry, 'an army beyond counting', but was roundly defeated, whereupon Hezekiah released Padi, who was put back on the throne of Ekron. Sennacherib continues:[1]

> As to Hezekiah, the Jew [rather, Judaean], he did not submit to my yoke, I laid siege to 46 of his strong cities, walled forts and to the countless small villages in their vicinity, and conquered (them) by means of well-stamped (earth-)ramps, and battering-rams brought near (to the walls), (combined with) the attack of foot soldiers (using) mines, breeches as well as sapper work. I drove out (of them) 200,150 people, young and old, male and female, horses, mules, donkeys, camels, big and small cattle beyond counting, and considered (them) booty. Himself I made a prisoner in Jerusalem, his royal residence, like a bird in a cage. I surrounded him with earthwork in order to molest those who were leaving his city's gate. His towns which I had plundered, I took away from his country and gave them to Mitinti, king of Ashdod, Padi, king of Ekron, and Sillibel, king of Gaza. Thus I reduced his country, but I still increased the tribute and the *katru*-presents (due) to me (as his) overlord which I imposed (later) upon him beyond the former tribute, to be delivered annually. Hezekiah himself, whom the terror-inspiring splendor of my lordship had overwhelmed and whose irregular and élite troops which he had brought into Jerusalem, his royal residence, in order to strengthen (it), had deserted, did send me, later, to Nineveh, my lordly city, together with 30 talents of gold, 800 talents of silver, precious stones, antimony, large cuts of red stone, couches (inlaid) with ivory, *nimedu*-chairs (inlaid) with ivory, elephant hides,

[1] *ANET*, p. 288.

ebony-wood, boxwood (and) all kinds of valuable treasures, his (own) daughters, concubines, male and female musicians. In order to deliver the tribute and to do obeisance as a slave he sent his (personal) messenger.

It will be noticed that Sennacherib does not claim to have captured Jerusalem nor to have carried out a wanton destruction of Judaean cities. He appears to have laid siege to a large number of fortified towns, including Jerusalem, and to have plundered what he captured, but he left the country together with his army as soon as Hezekiah gave up and accepted the heavy tribute laid upon him. According to 2 Kings 18. 14, Hezekiah did this when the Assyrian was encamped at the great Judaean fortress of Lachish.

Sennacherib was sufficiently proud of his conquest of Lachish to have a large picture of the event carved in low relief on stone and installed in his palace at Nineveh, where it was found a century ago. The relief shows the siege in progress and at the same time the fortress in process of surrender to Sennacherib in person. In front of the king is an inscription which reads: 'Sennacherib, king of the world, king of the land of Asshur, on the *nimedu*-chair, and the booty of the city of Lachish before him passed.'

Lachish was one of the major cities of Palestine at this time, larger even than Jerusalem and Megiddo. It was situated in the Judaean Lowlands (Shephelah), the chief fortress in a chain of north–south strongholds which had been fortified by Rehoboam at the end of the 10th century (2 Chr. 11. 5–10). The site was excavated between 1932 and 1938 by a British expedition under J. L. Starkey. We shall hear more about the important discoveries of this expedition at the end of the chapter, when we deal with the final destruction of Judah by the Babylonians. For the period of 701 B.C. two items are of special interest.

First, the city fortifications. The summit of the mound was surrounded by a brick wall. Over 50 feet below it along the slope of the mound was a stone-and-brick revetment. The two walls are clearly shown in the Lachish relief. One interesting object found buried in a mass of burnt debris at the base of the outer fortification was a bronze crest mount, once riveted to the top of a helmet. In the Lachish relief such crests are shown on the helmets of the Assyrian spearmen, but whether the object belonged to a member of Sennacherib's army or to a soldier of Nebuchadnezzar over a century later is unknown.

Secondly, there was found on the north-west slope of the mound a large pit which had once been a tomb, associated with five other smaller pits. They were filled with a conglomeration of bones, the jumbled remains of at least 150 bodies. Some of the bones and skulls showed signs of having been burned, and it is clear that the remains had been gathered up from some other area and thrown into this repository after the flesh had decomposed or been burned. Over the solid mass of human bones and spilling over into adjoining pits was a layer of animal bones, most of them from pigs! Along with the bones were many pieces of pottery, and some of the bowls and dishes were the type of vessel which is rarely found in tombs, though very common in the ruins of houses. In other words, this deposit was no ordinary cemetery. Mr. Starkey, the excavator, originally suggested that the deposit represented the clearance of the city after the siege of Sennacherib, and this explanation has much to commend it. It would explain the conglomerate nature of the deposit, the evidence of burning on some of the bones, and also the fact that few of the people buried here were old. One further interesting fact is that at least three of the skulls show evidence of the operation known as trepanning. They are the first specimens found in Western Asia, though others have since been found in Middle Bronze Age tombs at Jericho. On two of the skulls the crude saw marks are still so clear where the piece of bone was removed to relieve the pressure on the brain that we must presume that the patient died almost immediately. The bone of the third skull, on the other hand, had begun to grow again. The evidence of these skulls is a surprising testimony to the advanced state of Judaean medicine during the time of the prophet Isaiah. The presence of so many pig bones is also surprising in view of the Israelite dietary laws, which for good reason forbade the eating of pork. This prohibition did not extend to Israel's neighbors, however, and it is not impossible that the pigs at Lachish were brought there as part of the commissariat of the Assyrian Army.

In Jerusalem the only evidence which relates directly to Sennacherib's raid has to do with the city's water supply. 2 Kings 20. 20 speaks of how Hezekiah 'made the pool and the conduit and brought water into the city'. 2 Chr. 32. 30 says that he 'closed the upper outlet of the waters of Gihon and directed them down to the west side of the city of David'. The verses indicate that in preparation for a siege, presumably that of Sennacherib, the king arranged for the city to have an interior water supply. He prepared a new reservoir, the 'Pool of Siloam' (Isa. 22. 9, 11), within the city fortifications in the south-western quarter of the city. He then dug a tunnel under the hill to take the water from the Gihon to it, and evidently covered over the Gihon itself so that its presence would not be visible to the attackers. In 1880 some boys discovered an inscription in the tunnel about 25 feet from the Siloam end. This Siloam inscription has for many years been the most important monumental piece of writing in Israelite Palestine, and other Hebrew inscriptions have been dated by comparing the shapes of the letters with it. A flat surface had been prepared on the wall of the tunnel for the inscription, but only six lines on the lower part remain. These have been translated as follows:[1]

> [. . . when] (the tunnel) was driven through. And this is the way in which it was cut through:—While [. . .] (were) still (. . .) axe(s), each man toward his fellow, and while there were still three cubits to be cut through, [there was heard] the voice of a man calling to his fellow, for there was *an overlap* in the rock on the right [and on the left]. And when the tunnel was driven through, the quarrymen hewed (the rock), each man toward his fellow, axe against axe; and the water flowed from the spring toward the reservoir for 1,200 cubits, and the height of the rock above the head(s) of the quarrymen was 100 cubits.

Across the valley east of the Gihon and the mound where the old city of Jerusalem once stood is a rocky slope on which today stands the modern village of Silwan (Siloam). On this slope a number of ancient tombs still exist. The French archaeologist Clermont-Ganneau discovered one at the end of the last century which was different from the others. It was a rock-cut chamber with a dressed façade and a rectangular door, over which an inscription had been carved on a recessed panel. It was in such a badly damaged state, however, that its discoverer thought it had been defaced deliberately with a hammer.

[1] *ANET*, p. 321.

This inscription, 'the third longest monumental inscription in Hebrew and the first known text of a Hebrew sepulchral inscription from the pre-Exilic period', has only recently been deciphered, by Professor N. Avigad, of the Hebrew University in Jerusalem.[1] His translation is as follows:

> 1. This is [the sepulcher of . . .] yahu who is over the house.
> There is no silver and gold here
> 2. but [his bones] and the bones of his slave-wife with him.
> Cursed be the man.
> 3. who will open this!

The style of the epitaph corresponds closely to that of the Phoenicians (or Canaanites), and the details regarding the contents of the tomb have parallels in Syrian tomb inscriptions. Tomb-robbing was such a common ancient practice that the mere statement of a curse was insufficient; it was also explicitly stated that no valuables were present. Neither the statement nor the curse availed here, however, for the tomb has long been emptied of its contents.

The date of the epitaph cannot be long before or after about 700 B.C., because the manner in which the letters were formed is so similar to that of the Siloam inscription. Unfortunately a hole in the panel occurs precisely at the place where the name of the tomb's builder comes. All that we know is that his name ended in *yahu* (AV *iah*), and that he was a high royal official. One cannot but recall the passage in Isa. 22. 15 ff. where Isaiah excoriates the Prime Minister of the early part of Hezekiah's reign, 'Shebna,

[1] *Israel Exploration Journal*, III (1953), pp. 137–152.

who is over the house', for hewing himself out a tomb in the rock, 'on the height', presumably in plain sight of the city and probably in the very area where the tomb described above is. It has long been known that the name Shebna is an abbreviation for *Shebanyahu* (Shebaniah). The tomb discussed here was built during the owner's lifetime; otherwise the builder would not have said that the bones of his favourite concubine or slave-wife were buried with his own. Thus the combination of date, place, and content of the tomb's epitaph suggest that it may indeed have been that of Shebna.

Judah during the 7th Century

Manasseh, Hezekiah's son and successor (*c.* 687–642 B.C.), attempted to turn the religion of Yahwism into another polytheism. Accepting the planet- and star-worship of his Assyrian conquerors, he erected altars for the pagan deities in the very courts of Yahweh's 'house'. This means that he encouraged the people to think of the pagan gods as members of Yahweh's heavenly host, associated with him in both the heavenly and earthly temples.

The Assyrian emperors during Manasseh's reign were Esarhaddon (681–669 B.C.) and Asshurbanapal (669–*c.* 633 B.C.). They accomplished the conquest of Egypt during the seventies and sixties of the century, and the fall of Thebes, the great city of upper Egypt, in 663 B.C. was still remembered by the Judaean prophet Nahum many years later ('No' in Nah. 3. 8 was a name of the city). Both these kings mention Manasseh in their inscriptions. Esarhaddon leaves us a list of twelve kings along the Mediterranean sea-coast whom he forced to supply the wood and stone for his palace at Nineveh. Manasseh is referred to as *Manasi* King of *Yaudi*. Asshurbanapal gives a similar list of kings, referring to them as 'servants who belong to me', and saying that he made them accompany his army on its journey through their territory and supply troops and ships to assist him. In each case Manasseh is second in the list, after the King of Tyre; he thus held an important place among the kings of Syria and Palestine.

From the late 8th or early 7th century an undated Assyrian text mentions the tribute sent by the kingdoms of Ammon, Moab, Judah, and Edom. Judah's contribution, ten minas of silver, could not have been a heavy tribute, though we do not know how often such an amount would be required. According to present reckoning, a Mesopotamian mina, composed of 60 shekels, as opposed to the Syro-Palestinian mina of 50 shekels, would have weighed approximately 685 grams. Ten minas of silver in Mesopotamia would thus be equivalent to the amount of metal in about 255 silver dollars. The purchasing power of this sum would, of course, have been far greater than it is today. For example, during the final siege of Jerusalem Jeremiah bought a field for 17 shekels of silver (Jer. 32. 9), which would be equivalent to the weight of the metal in 7 silver dollars. On the other hand, one part only of the tribute imposed on Hezekiah by Sennacherib was 800 talents of silver, which would be the same as 48,000 minas or the weight of 1,224,000 silver dollars.

Between 652 and 647 B.C. a serious revolt against Assyria occurred, led by Babylon. This would have been the most natural occasion for the revolt of Manasseh as described in 2 Chr. 33. 11, though we have no other information about it. It seems probable that the Arab tribes of the Syrian desert took this occasion to press into eastern Syria and Transjordan. Asshurbanapal gives considerable space in his annals to his struggle against the Arabs, whom he had to fight in Transjordan. The remarkable lament over the fall of Moab, preserved in Isa. 15–16, was probably occasioned by the Arab inundations of Transjordan during this century.

The most remarkable Judaean monarch of the century was Manasseh's grandson Josiah (*c.* 640–609 B.C.). 2 Chr. 34. 3 says that in the 8th year of his reign (633–632 B.C.) the king 'began to seek the God of David his father'; that is, he repudiated the gods of his Assyrian rulers and turned squarely against the syncretistic policies of his grandfather. This action probably followed immediately upon the death of Asshurbanapal.

A more drastic move was made in the period of disorder which followed the death of Asshurbanapal's successor, Asshuretelilani, about 629 B.C. 2 Chr. 34. 3–7 says that it took place in Josiah's 12th year (629–628 B.C.) and that it was a thorough-going reform in which all idolatrous altars and images were destroyed, not only in Judah, but also throughout the territory of Israel as far as Galilee. Such a purge is unthinkable without military control over the Assyrian provinces of Samaria and Megiddo. In other words, Josiah, probably as a nominal vassal of Assyria, was reasserting the ancient Davidic claim to a united Palestine by annexing the northern Assyrian provinces.

In 628–627, during Josiah's 13th year, Jeremiah received his call to be God's prophet (Jer. 1. 2). His early prophecies about the northern peril, together with those of his contemporary Zephaniah, have been interpreted by many scholars in the past as occasioned by a great invasion of Scythian hordes from Armenia and southern Russia. This supposition is based solely upon an unverified statement of Herodotus, the 5th-century Greek historian, who claimed that the Scythians invaded Western Asia at this time and ruled over it for 'eight-and-twenty years, during which time their insolence and oppression spread ruin on every side'.[1] That the Scythians were a serious trouble to the Assyrians along their northern border seems to have been true, but, as we reconstruct the history of the time from archaeological sources, there is no room or evidence for the Scythian domination of which Herodotus speaks. In any event, the decline of Assyria and the rising hope of Judah after Josiah's action would have been sufficient to account for the early proclamations of Jeremiah and Zephaniah, to both of whom the breakdown of world order meant that the Day of the Lord as a day of judgment was at hand.

The finding of the old lawbook in the Temple (some part of Deuteronomy) during the 18th year of Josiah's reign (*c*. 623–622 B.C.) resulted in a still more thorough-going religious reform, in which all sacrificial worship was confined to the Jerusalem Temple (2 Kings 22–23). The reform probably signalled the final break with Assyria. We know that by 623 B.C. Assyrian control over Babylonia had ceased entirely, and that a Babylonian king, Nabopolassar, had consolidated his position and was preparing to attack Assyria itself.

In 1923 C. J. Gadd of the British Museum published a portion of the Babylonian Chronicle. This document gives a detailed summary, year by year, of the fall of the Assyrian Empire. The climax came in 612 B.C., when the capital, Nineveh, fell to the combined forces of the Medes and the Babylonians. The Assyrian king and his army withdrew into northern Mesopotamia. In 609 or 608 B.C. they were finally crushed by the Babylonians with the aid

[1] *History*, Book I, Chapters 104–106.

of the Medes in the Battle of Haran. From the Babylonian Chronicle we learn that the Pharaoh Necho of Egypt went to the aid of the Assyrians (not to fight against them as in 2 Kings 23. 29 AV; see RSV), Josiah opposed him and was killed by him at Megiddo. Necho was interested in regaining Palestine and Syria for Egypt, and it would have been to his advantage to have had a weak Assyria as a buffer against the Babylonians. Josiah was anti-Assyrian, and he must have known that with Necho in control of Syria and Palestine the newly erected state of united Israel could not survive. His only hope was so to delay the forces of Necho by making them deploy for siege that they would not arrive in time at Haran. This he succeeded in doing, though at the cost of his life.

The archaeological evidence for the siege of Megiddo, which resulted in Josiah's death, is the destruction of the city of Stratum II at that site. After the battle between Necho and Josiah Megiddo was never again an important place. For some two and a half centuries it remained a small and perhaps unfortified village. In the 4th century B.C. the mound was abandoned entirely.

Nebuchadnezzar

Pharaoh Necho was able to control Syria and Palestine until his crushing defeat by Nebuchadnezzar of Babylon at the Battle of Carchemish in northern Syria in 605 B.C. During the following years the armies of Babylon advanced to the border of Egypt, rolling the last vestiges of Necho's power from Asia. Jehoiakim of Judah promptly submitted and remained loyal for a time before rebelling (2 Kings 24. 1). A neighboring king did not submit so readily. This we learn from an Aramaic letter found at Saqqara in Egypt in 1942 and first published in 1948.

After the salutation the letter reads, according to the reconstruction of H. L. Ginsberg:[1]

> That [I have written to my lord is to inform thee that the troops] of the king of Babylon have advanced as far as Aphek and have begun to . . . they have taken. . . . For the Lord of Kingdoms, Pharaoh knows that [thy] servant [cannot stand alone against the king of Babylon. May it therefore please him] to send a force to succor m[e for thy servant is loyal to my lord] and thy servant remembers his kindness, and this region [is my lord's possession. But if the king of Babylon takes it, he will set up] a governor in the land and . . .

In other words Nebuchadnezzar's army has reached Aphek (modern Ras el-'Ain, just north-east of Joppa). Adon, who sends the letter, must be king therefore of a city south of there, presumably one of the five great cities of the Philistines (Gaza, Ashkelon, Ashdod, Ekron, and Gath). Ashkelon is the best possibility. That Ashkelon was taken by Nebuchadnezzar is confirmed by the judgment pronounced against it by Jeremiah (Jer. 47. 5, 7), and also by the fact that Babylonian tablets of ten years later mention among the captives living in Babylon two royal princes of Ashkelon, and Ashkelonian foremen and seamen.

There is another reason for the importance of the letter. It is one of the oldest Aramaic papyri known and the first evidence that Aramaic was supplanting Akkadian as the international diplomatic language. We know that Aramaic was the official language of the Persian empire, and that as early as 700 B.C. highly placed persons could converse in the tongue (2 Kings 18. 26) and use it in business. Yet before the discovery of this letter it had not been

[1] *BASOR*, No. 111 (1948), pp. 24–27.

dreamed that Akkadian was being displaced so early in diplomacy.

It was in 599 B.C. that Jehoiakim, King of Judah, rebelled against Nebuchadnezzar, bringing retaliation from the latter in 598 B.C. Less than ten years later Judah again rebelled under Zedekiah, and this time, in 589–587 B.C., Nebuchadnezzar laid the country waste completely, bringing all life and commerce to a virtual standstill. Evidence for the two invasions is to be seen most clearly in the ruins of two Judaean fortresses which protected the hill country. These are Debir and Lachish. At Debir in 598 the Babylonian army seems to have destroyed both of the city gates and the fortress in the center, but most of the town escaped demolition. In the second invasion, however, the city was completely destroyed, buildings and fortifications pulled down and burned, so that the site was never reoccupied. Precisely the same seems to have happened at Lachish. In 598 B.C. the city gate, fortifications, and palace-citadel seem to have been destroyed; and in 589–588 B.C. the city was completely demolished. As a result the site was deserted and not reoccupied until nearly a century and a half later.

Nebuchadnezzar does not mention these events in any of his surviving inscriptions, probably because it was not Babylonian custom to brag about military exploits in the way the Assyrian emperors had done. Instead, the Babylonian was inclined to tell about the good deeds he had performed for the gods in building and repairing temples, and the like. Apart from the Bible, our main source of information about the Neo-Babylonian Empire has been the Babylonian Chronicle, an official document which simply recorded the chief events year by year. In 1956 the discovery of four more tablets of the Chronicle was announced by D. J. Wiseman of the British Museum. They are especially important in that for the first time outside the Bible Nebuchadnezzar's capture of Jerusalem in 598–597 B.C. is described, while itemized information about other events between 626 and 594 B.C. is given, with a break in the text of only six years.

The following information in particular from the newly discovered documents may be mentioned: In 605 B.C. Nebuchadnezzar not only defeated the Egyptian Necho at Carchemish; we are told that he completely annihilated the army so that scarcely a man survived. Yet he was prevented from following up his advantage immediately because the death of his father in Babylon made it necessary for him to return home to be crowned. Hitherto unknown is the record of a major battle with the Egyptians in 601 B.C., in which Nebuchadnezzar was defeated. It was probably on the eve of this battle that the King of Ashkelon wrote his Aramaic letter to the Pharaoh for help. Furthermore, Nebuchadnezzar's defeat at this time makes it easier to understand why the Judaean king Jehoiakim revolted so soon afterwards. We are informed that Nebuchadnezzar in the 7th year of his reign marched his army into the land of Khatti (Syria–Palestine) and besieged Jerusalem. He captured the city on the 2nd day of the 12th month of his 7th year (mid-March 597 B.C.) and took the king prisoner. This not only confirms the biblical story: it also places the chronology of the period on a firmer footing. The final siege of Jerusalem (2 Kings 25. 1–7; cf. Jer. 52. 28–29) must have taken place between December–January 589–588 and July–August 587. The dates 597 and 587 now seem established for the two Babylonian captures of Jerusalem.

In 1939 Dr. Ernst F. Weidner, then of Berlin, published

a few of nearly 300 tablets which had been found years before in the ruins of a vaulted building supposed to have been the substructure of the Hanging Gardens of Babylon. The tablets list payments of rations in oil and grain from the Government to captives and skilled workmen from many nations who were living in Babylon between the years 595 and 570 B.C. Yaukin (Jehoiachin), King of Judah, five royal princes, and other Judaeans are listed, together with the royal princes of Ashkelon and mariners, musicians, shipbuilders, craftsmen, horse-trainers, and monkey-trainers from Egypt, Phoenicia, Asia Minor, and Iran. One of the documents mentioning Jehoiachin is dated 592 B.C.

This evidence suggests that Jehoiachin was being held as a hostage for the good behaviour of the Judaeans and that he was considered the true king. His uncle Zedekiah, whom Nebuchadnezzar had put on the throne in Jerusalem, would then have been a type of regent. Certainly many Judaeans considered Jehoiachin the true king, who might return at any time (Jer. 28–29; and note that the framework of the book of Ezekiel is provided by a series of dates reckoned by the captivity of Jehoiachin). It is no surprise, then, to discover that the line of the Messiah was traced through him (Matt. 1. 11–12) and not through Zedekiah.

Further confirmation of the status of Jehoiachin in Babylon comes from the discovery in Palestine of three stamped jar-handles, which bore the words, 'Belonging to Eliakim, steward of Yaukin'. Two were found at Debir and one at Beth-shemesh. All three were made from the same original stamp-seal. This indicates that between 598 and 587 B.C. a person named Eliakim was the steward of the crown property of Jehoiachin when the latter was in captivity, that this property was kept intact and not appropriated by Zedekiah.

The most important single discovery from the last days of Judah is that of the Lachish Letters. Eighteen pieces of broken pottery on which letters and lists had hastily been written were found by Mr. Starkey in 1935 in the burnt debris of a guardroom in the city gate. In 1938 three more were discovered, one on the roadway and two in a room on the mound near the palace. Most of the letters are in a bad state of preservation, and only about one-third of them are fairly intelligible. In the words of W. F. Albright: 'Since they form the only known corpus of documents in classical Hebrew prose, they have unusual philological significance, quite aside from the light which they shed on the time of Jeremiah.'[1]

Most of the documents were notes written by one Hoshaiah to Yaosh, the commander of the Judaean forces at Lachish. Hoshaiah appears to have been in charge of an outpost north of Lachish, in a position where he could see the signals of Azekah, a city guarding the Vale of Elah in the Shephelah to the north. In Letter IV he writes: 'And let (my lord) know that we are watching for the signals of Lachish, according to all the indications which my lord have given, for we cannot see Azekah.' The situation may be that depicted in Jer. 34. 7, when Lachish and Azekah were the only fortified cities that had not been taken. When Hoshaiah says that he 'cannot see Azekah' he may mean that the latter city has already fallen and is no longer sending signals. A date in the autumn of 589 (or 588) B.C. has been suggested for the bulk of the letters. On Letter XX are the words 'the ninth year' (of King Zedekiah).

[1] *ANET*, p. 322. The translations below are from the same source.

That is the same year in which Nebuchadnezzar arrived to begin the reduction of Judah (2 Kings 25. 1).

Judah revolted against Nebuchadnezzar because of the usual promise of help from Egypt. It was probably in reference to the matter of Egyptian aid that Hoshaiah says in Letter III: 'And it hath been reported to thy servant, saying, "The commander of the host, Coniah son of Elnathan, hath come down in order to go into Egypt; and unto Hodaviah son of Ahijah and his men hath he sent to obtain . . . from him."' Hoshaiah continues: 'And as for the letter of Tobiah, servant of the king, which came to Shallum son of Jaddua through the prophet, saying, "Beware!" thy servant hath sent it to my lord.' Who the prophet was that acted as the bearer of the letter we do not know of course, but the documents make it clear that important letters were widely circulated, and it is of interest to note Hoshaiah's detailed explanation of the way in which he received the letter he was about to forward. Letter XVI has another reference to 'the prophet', but only the *ahu* (AV *iah*) at the end of his name is preserved. He has been identified with Uriah (Jer. 26. 20) and also with Jeremiah, but there were doubtless many prophets whose names ended in this way.

In Letter VI the princes or royal officials are accused of 'weakening' the hands of the army and the people, which is precisely what the same princes accused Jeremiah of doing (Jer. 38. 4):

> To my lord Yaosh: May Yahweh cause my lord to see this season in good health. Who is thy servant (but) a dog that my lord hath sent the [let]ter of the king and the letters of the prince[s, say]ing, 'Pray read them!' And behold the words of the pr[inces] are not good (but)

> to weaken our hands [and to sla]cken the hands of the *m[en] who are informed about them* [. . . . And now] my lord, wilt thou not write to them, saying, 'Why do ye thus [*even*] in Jerusalem? Behold unto the king and unto [*his house*] are ye doing this thing!' [And,] as Yahweh thy God liveth, truly since thy servant read the letters there hath been no [*peace*] for [thy ser]vant. . . .

From Jerusalem no archaeological evidence of the Babylonian destruction has been recovered. Yet we can have no doubt that the devastation was as complete as the book of Lamentations suggests that it was. The violence visited upon Judah is clear not only from the excavations of such sites as Lachish, Debir, and Beth-shemesh but also from surveys which show that city after city ceased to be inhabited at this time, many never to be reoccupied. It was two centuries before a numerous population with a degree of prosperity had resettled the land.

Maps, Texts, and Illustrations

Maps

WHA, Plates VIIC, XIA, B, XVIIA, XVIII; Grollenberg, Maps 19–20

Texts

(p. 109) Sennacherib's siege of Jerusalem: *ANE*, 199–201; *ANET*, 287–8; *DOTT*, 64–9

(p. 110) The Lachish Relief: *DOTT*, 69–70

(p. 113) The Siloam Inscription: *ANE*, 212; *ANET*, 321; *DOTT*, 209–11

(p. 115) The Assyrian kings and Manasseh: *ANE*, 201–2; *ANET*, 291, 294; *DOTT*, 73–5

(p. 116) The tribute text: *ANE*, 202; *ANET*, 301
(p. 116) Asshurbanapal and the Arabs: *ANET*, 297–301
(pp. 118, 121) The Babylonian Chronicle: *ANE*, 202–3; *ANET*, 303–5; *DOTT*. 75–83
(p. 119) The Saqqara Letter: *DOTT*, 251–5
(p. 122) The Jehoiachin Tablets: *ANET*, 308; *DOTT*, 84–6
(p. 124) The Lachish Letters: *ANE*, 212–14; *ANET*, 321–2; *DOTT*, 212–7

Illustrations (The references are to figures)

(p. 109) The Sennacherib Prism: *DOTT*, 4; Grollenberg, 248; Wiseman, 54; Wright, 114
(p. 110) The Lachish Relief: *ANE*, 101–2; *ANEP*, 371–4; Wiseman, 57; Wright, 115–7; *WHA* (5th ed.), 36
(p. 111) Assyrian soldier's crest: *ANEP*, 175; Wright, 119
(p. 112) Trepanning: Wright, 120
(p. 112) Hezekiah's Tunnel: *ANEP*, 744; Grollenberg, 231; Wiseman, 55; Wright, 121
(p. 113) The Siloam Inscription: *ANE*, 73; *ANEP*, 275; *DOTT*, 11; Grollenberg, 232; Wiseman, 56; Wright, 122
(p. 113) 'Shebna's' Tomb: Wiseman, 53; Wright, 123
(p. 121) The Babylonian Chronicle: *ANE*, 59; *DOTT*, 5; Wiseman, 63
(p. 122) The Jehoiachin Tablets: Wiseman, 69
(p. 123) The Eliakim Seal: *ANE*, 77; *ANEP*, 278; *DOTT* (p. 224); Wright, 125
(p. 124) The Lachish Letters: *ANE*, 80; *ANEP*, 279; *DOTT*, 12; Wiseman, 64

CHAPTER VIII

AFTER THE EXILE

Archaeological evidence to illumine the life of the Jewish community which slowly came into being in the 6th and following centuries is far less extensive than it is for earlier periods. Consequently in this chapter we shall not only survey the main discoveries which bear upon the history of the period but we shall also review briefly a few items that throw light on the sacred literature, which in this age was attaining its final form.

The Palestinian Community: 6th–4th Centuries B.C.

So thorough was Nebuchadnezzar's destruction of Judah that many years pass by before evidence of reoccupation can be detected. In fact, the country's recovery to its former prosperity was very slow and extended over a period of three centuries; and the new Judaean community was established, not in the whole of its former territory, but in a comparatively small area around Jerusalem.

North of Jerusalem four towns in particular show evidence of continued occupation during the 6th century. This supports the inference from the narrative in 2 Kings that Nebuchadnezzar confined his attention to Judah and Jerusalem and did not lay waste areas to the north. These towns are Tell en-Nasbeh (Mizpah?), Bethel, Samaria, and Megiddo. None of them yield objects or architecture of especial interest from this time, nor do they show any evidence of economic vigor. Indeed, a portion of the mound at Samaria seems to have been purposely covered with earth from the surrounding hillsides so that it could be used as an orchard or vineyard. Bethel was destroyed and abandoned some time before 500 B.C., but we cannot be certain who was responsible. The town was subsequently resettled and continued to be occupied into the Roman period. Tell en-Nasbeh and Megiddo were destroyed and abandoned in the 4th century. Of all the excavated sites of Palestine, Samaria alone has revealed a fairly continuous occupation throughout the period from the fall of Jerusalem through inter-testamental and New Testament times. It is small wonder, then, that our archaeological knowledge of the post-exilic and inter-testamental ages is so fragmentary. This very fact is eloquent testimony to the hardships and privations which the decimated population of the country had to undergo.

The new Judaean community, established during the 6th and 5th centuries, was confined to a small area, extending less than 25 miles along the central ridge, from a few miles north of Jerusalem to Beth-zur, north of Hebron. Its population by 440 B.C. was reckoned at less than 50,000 (Neh. 7. 66 ff.), and it was surrounded by hostile and troublesome neighbors. That it was established at all was due to a radically new policy in the treatment of subject peoples which was initiated by the Persian king Cyrus. In an inscription written for publication in Babylon after its capture in 539 B.C., Cyrus describes how he was able to take the city and what he did after seizing it. He claims that Marduk, the lord of the gods of Babylon, had become angered at the impious acts of the king of the country, Nabonidus. The latter was 'a weakling' who interfered improperly with religious affairs, blabbering incorrect prayers, interrupting the regular offerings, and changing the worship of Marduk into an abomination. This god searched through all countries for 'a righteous ruler', chose Cyrus, and declared him ruler of the world. As a result, Cyrus entered Babylon without a battle, spared the city calamity, and immediately turned his attention to the alleviation of the people's complaints. He then reversed the policy of his Assyrian and Babylonian predecessors of deporting people from their homelands and forcing them to live elsewhere. He says that he gathered all the former inhabitants of the various countries, 'returned (to them) their habitations', rebuilt their sanctuaries, and returned the images of their gods which had been taken away.

This information enables us to place the Judaean return from Babylonian exile in its proper setting. Ezra 1. 2–4 and 6. 3–5 preserve two accounts of the decree of Cyrus permitting the return and the rebuilding of the Temple in Jerusalem. The second is in Aramaic and has generally been considered more reliable than the first, which is in Hebrew, though some scholars have been inclined to doubt the authenticity of them both. Recently the two documents have received careful study in the light of our present knowledge of royal decrees in the ancient world, particularly in the time of the Persian Empire. The result is to the effect that there is no reason to doubt the substantial authenticity of either account. The second is explicitly entitled a *dikrona*, an official Aramaic term for a memorandum which recorded an oral decision of the king or other official and which initiated administrative action. It was never intended for publication but solely for the eye of the proper official and then for filing in the government archives. According to Ezra 6, it was found in the government archive building at Ecbatana, where Cyrus stayed during the summer of his first year as king (538 B.C.). The Hebrew document (Ezra 1. 2–4) was of a different type. It was a royal proclamation made throughout the empire to all Judaeans. Whereas official letters and documents were generally in Aramaic, verbal proclamation was of necessity in the national language of those addressed.

It has been objected to the decree in this form that Cyrus would scarcely speak as though he were a convert of the God of Israel: 'Yahweh, the God of heaven, has given me all the kingdoms of the earth, and he has charged me to build him a house at Jerusalem.' Yet this was precisely his method. We have already noted that in the Babylonian inscription the king says virtually the same about Marduk as he says here about Yahweh.

During the 6th century the political leaders of the new Judah were descendants of the Davidic house, and many Jews dreamed of the re-establishment of a state ruled by the Davidic dynasty. These hopes were not fulfilled, however, and henceforward the province of Judah was ruled internally by the high priest, while foreign affairs were the concern of a governor appointed by the Persian court. The most famous of these governors was Nehemiah, a Judaean layman who had become an official in the court of Artaxerxes I (465–424 B.C.) and who held office in Jerusalem during the third quarter of the 5th century. From his time through the 4th century the province had the status of a semi-autonomous priestly commonwealth, similar to that of Hierapolis in northern Syria, with the right to levy its own taxes and issue its own coinage.

Four groups of seal impressions on jar-handles of the 5th and 4th centuries, bearing the names 'Judah', 'Jerusalem', and *msh* (Mozah?) indicate a local autonomy in fiscal matters and the attempt by the province and its capital city to regulate business life and the collection of taxes. This was done by licensing certain potters to use official stamps on jars of guaranteed capacity. During the second half of the 5th and during the 4th century coins with Hebrew letters on them appear in Judah. Several of them bear the letters of the name of the province, *Yehud*. The existence of these coins indicates that the province of Judah had been given considerable local autonomy, with the right to strike its own coinage.

Exiles in Mesopotamia and Egypt

The prophet Ezekiel, during his exile in Babylonia, lived in or near the town of Tel-abib on the River Chebar. The latter, called Kabar by the Babylonians, was one of the large irrigation canals. We do not know precisely where Tel-abib was, but the name is good Babylonian, *til-abubu*, meaning 'Mound of the Flood'. During this time towns with names beginning *til* (Hebrew *tel*) were very common, for many old tells or mounds, long unoccupied, were being resettled.

The one city in Babylonia which we know from excavation to have had a Jewish colony was Nippur, south-east of Babylon. Here the archives of a great Babylonian firm of bankers and brokers of the 5th century were discovered. The large number of Hebrew names leaves us in no doubt that many of the exiles from Judah had been settled in this area, and that while the returned exiles were attempting to rebuild Jerusalem, others stayed in Babylonia and prospered. Indeed, many inscribed Hebrew bowls suggest that a colony of Jews lived in Nippur for centuries.

The evidence for Jewish settlement in Egypt comes from the Elephantine papyri, discovered on an island in the

Nile. During the 5th century Elephantine was a fortress called Yeb, garrisoned by a colony of Jews, who had erected a temple there. We learn from recently published letters [1] that the Persian satrap or governor of Egypt, Arsham or Arsames, was absent from Egypt in Babylon and Susa between 410 and 408 B.C., and that during his absence there were disturbances in Egypt. One of the Elephantine papyri is a copy of a letter sent by the priests of the Jewish temple at Yeb to Bagoas, the governor of Judah, telling him that the temple has been destroyed and asking his aid in having it rebuilt. The letter was written in 407 B.C., and says that in July 410 B.C., when Arsames had left Egypt, the priests of a local Egyptian temple conspired with a 'wretch' named Vidaranag to raze and burn the rival Jewish temple. It was an old and honored building, dating 'back in the days of the kingdom of Egypt', before the Persian Cambyses had conquered the country, that is, before 525 B.C. The Jewish priests complain that they had written to Johanan, the high priest of the Jerusalem temple (Neh. 12. 22–23), but that they had received no answer. They have also written to Delaiah and Shelemiah, the sons of Sanballat, governor of Samaria.

An undated memorandum would indicate that answers were received from both Delaiah and Bagoas, who advised that a petition be addressed directly to Arsames about the matter. A copy of this petition has been recovered, signed by five Jews who say that they are property-owners in the fortress. It states that no animal sacrifice will be offered if permission is given for the rebuilding of the temple, 'but (only) incense, meal-offering, [and drink-offering]'.[2] We do

[1] See G. R. Driver, *Aramaic Documents of the Fifth Century B.C.* (Oxford, 1954; abridged and revised edition, 1957).

[2] *ANET*, p. 492.

not know why the Jewish community at Elephantine were careful to state that no animals were to be sacrificed there if the temple was erected again. It is likely that the Jews had been advised to make this concession in order not to rouse opposition from Jerusalem and from the commissioner of Jewish affairs in the chancery of Arsames. The 'Passover Papyrus' of 419 B.C., some years earlier, was a letter to the community from such a commissioner, stating that Arsames was ordering the Passover to be celebrated at Yeb according to certain precise regulations. These regulations accord with Pentateuchal law, which suggests that the order of Arsames was an attempt to secure uniformity in Jewish practice under pressure from the priesthood in Jerusalem. At any rate, we know from documents in the Brooklyn Museum [1] that the temple was rebuilt; the Elephantine compromise was therefore effective.

The very existence of a Jewish temple in Egypt points to a type of Jewish worship which the Jerusalem priests at this time would certainly have considered heterodox. After the reform of King Josiah in 622 B.C. it was considered unlawful for animal sacrifices to be made on any altar except that in Jerusalem. Further indication of heterodoxy is to be found in one of the papyri which list the contributors to the temple and their contributions. In the final reckoning one portion is set aside for the worship of *Yahu* (the name of the God of Israel as it was spelt by these Jews), a second portion for a deity named *Ishumbethel*, and a third for *Anathbethel*.[2] The second of these divine names means 'name of the house of God'. The third either refers to the Canaanite fertility goddess Anath or else it means 'sign of

[1] See E. G. Kraeling, *The Brooklyn Museum Aramaic Papyri* (New Haven, 1953).
[2] *ANET*, p. 491.

the house of God'. Another document makes reference to *Anath-Yahu*. This, when taken with *Anathbethel*, seems to suggest that *bethel* was used as a divine name and as a substitute for *Yahu*. Still another document mentions *Herembethel*, perhaps 'sacredness of the house of God'.

The interpretation of these divine names has caused much discussion among scholars. One view is simply that though the Jews at Elephantine worshipped *Yahu* as the national god, they borrowed other deities from the Canaanite and Aramaean environment and worshipped them also. It is more probable, however, that these Jews were personifying certain qualities or aspects of Yahweh. Pagan religions had been doing this for some time, especially as regards the Word which issues from a deity's mouth. In any case, the Jews at Elephantine were developing a somewhat questionable type of Jewish faith under pagan influence.

It was noted above that the high priest in Jerusalem about 410 B.C., when the Egyptian temple was destroyed, was Johanan. When Nehemiah returned to Jerusalem about 445 B.C. the high priest was Eliashib (Neh. 3. 1). His successors were Joiada, Johanan, and Jaddua (Neh. 12. 22). When Ezra returned to Jerusalem, he went to the chamber of Johanan (or Jehohanan), to issue a proclamation calling all Judaeans to a provincial assembly (Ezra 10. 6–8). Many scholars believe that Johanan must have been high priest at that time, because such a directive would be issued only from the high priest's office. Yet Johanan was after Nehemiah's time, as we have seen, and if the Johanan in Ezra 10. 6–8 was high priest, then Ezra must have followed Nehemiah instead of preceding him, as the Chronicler assumed. For this reason and others, perhaps a majority of scholars today believe that Ezra came to

Jerusalem in the 7th year of Artaxerxes II (Ezra 7. 7; 398 B.C.), not of Artaxerxes I (458 B.C.), or sometime after 432 B.C., that is, at the end of the reign of Artaxerxes I.

These documents have made possible a much greater knowledge of the Aramaic language of the 5th century, the official tongue of the Persian Empire and the one which most people between Babylon and Egypt then spoke. Before these discoveries the Aramaic portions of the book of Ezra (4. 8–6, 18; 7. 12–26), which include transcripts of what purport to be official documents of the Persian Government, had no contemporary witness by which they could be validated and understood. Now, however, we are able to see that the Aramaic of Ezra is precisely that of its age, while the government documents are of the general type which we have become accustomed to associate with the Persian regime.

Palestine in the Hellenistic Age

The Persian Empire fell to the Greek conqueror, Alexander the Great, in 333–331 B.C., but that ruler's death in 323 B.C. brought to an end his dream of uniting east and west in one great brotherhood, dominated by Greek culture. The empire was divided among his generals, and Palestine became the border country between the Seleucid dynasty of Syria and the Ptolemies of Egypt. Throughout the 3rd century and until 198 B.C. it was controlled by Egypt. Then the Seleucids seized the country and attempted to unite it with Syria under a Hellenistic culture, with a mixed Greek and Syrian religion, Greek language, literature, sports, and dress. The movement reached its peak under Antiochus IV or Epiphanes (175–163 B.C.), who attempted to destroy Judaism and convert the Temple into a place where the pagan god Zeus was worshipped. This initiated the Jewish Maccabaean revolt, and turned the 2nd century B.C. into one of bloody turmoil. The period of Jewish independence ended in 63 B.C., when the Romans took control of the country.

Such archaeological information as we have for this period comes for the most part from four cities. The first of these, Marisa (the Old Testament Mareshah, the modern Tell Sandahannah), had replaced Lachish as the chief city of Idumaea, and vividly illustrates the process of hellenization. It was built like a well-planned Greek town, with streets running at right angles and forming blocks of houses, while the market-place or agora next to the gate was rectangular, open at one end, with carefully built shops around three sides.

A second town of importance in this period is Beth-zur, north of Hebron, the scene of several battles during the Maccabaean wars of the 2nd century. A fortress was built there, probably during the Persian period, when the relations between Judah and Idumaea were tense. This was rebuilt into a much more elaborate structure by Judas Maccabaeus between 165 and 163 B.C. as an outpost against the Syrians. It was captured, however, and presumably destroyed and rebuilt on a Hellenistic plan by the pagan general Bacchides about 161 B.C.

From the 3rd century onwards, Samaria was a pagan city with a population which was largely foreign. About the time of Alexander the Great the old Israelite fortification walls had been repaired and strengthened, with the addition of several beautifully built round towers. About 150 B.C. a new wall round the summit of the mound was erected, evidently as a defense against the Maccabees. Remains of a small temple of about the 3rd century have also been recovered: it was probably destroyed about 108 B.C.

by John Hyrcanus, who had also captured and destroyed the main Samaritan metropolis, Shechem.

Finally, the great city of Gezer, in the foothills south-east of Joppa, was fortified by the Maccabees about 140 B.C. It apparently had a large Jewish population at the time, and in rocks around the city the legend 'Boundary of Gezer' had been cut in Hebrew or Aramaic characters, perhaps referring to the limits of a sabbath day's journey.

The cultural changes which had taken place since the destruction of Jerusalem had been so extensive that there were now few reminders of the time when Israel controlled the whole country. The things in common use, such as lamps, utensils, and jewelry, had all changed radically. Architecture became increasingly hellenized, and the country was filled with foreigners, a few of whom were to become famous as philosophers and scholars. The Jewish community itself was divided, and many Jews were by no means sympathetic to the Maccabaean revolt. The dispersion of the Jews over the world continued, and the first translation of the Hebrew Bible into Greek (the Septuagint) took place during the 3rd and 2nd centuries in Alexandria, at that time the intellectual center of the world. Palestine was the bridge between Asia and Egypt, and thus at the crossroads of the world, and the archaeological remains are an eloquent testimony to the fact.

The Old Testament

During the period under survey in this chapter the literature of the Old Testament was brought virtually into the form in which we now have it. Even the idea of a canon of sacred scripture emerged, though its exact limits were not yet precisely defined. It is believed that the Pentateuch was finished by the time of Ezra, and with the work of the Chronicler in the early 4th century the whole collection of historical material was completed. By the 4th century also the canon of the prophets and the books of Psalms, Proverbs, and Job had virtually reached their final form. By the time of Alexander the Great, then, we have only the books of Ecclesiastes, Esther, Song of Songs, and Daniel left to be accounted for.

The service which archaeology is rendering the study of Old Testament literature is threefold. (1) It has occasionally revealed literary parallels and background to biblical works. (2) It has unearthed ancient inscriptions in such numbers as to enable scholars to trace the history of the Hebrew language and script. (3) It has uncovered ancient biblical manuscripts which have revolutionized our study of the Hebrew text.

Pagan peoples of the day produced no literature which can be compared precisely with the historical and prophetic writings of the Old Testament. On the other hand, the study of ancient poetry, particularly that of the Canaanites from Ras Shamra, has been of invaluable assistance in the study of certain Hebrew poetic forms, vocabulary, and allusions. This study, together with other evidence, has reversed the tendency on the part of earlier scholars to date the composition of most of the Psalms in the post-exilic and even Maccabaean periods.

The book of Proverbs shows a closer relation to pagan literature than any other book in the Bible. Gnomic literature was one of the most international and ancient of the literary forms of the biblical world. Egyptian wisdom in particular has long been known; some of it is very close in type to the material in Proverbs. Indeed, it has long been suspected that there is a connection between the Egyptian

Wisdom of Amen-em-opet and Prov. 22. 17–24. 22, though the precise relationship is difficult to prove.

The book of Job has no close parallel in form, style, or penetration of thought. Yet its theme, the problem of the good man who suffers, is a very old one. There are several Mesopotamian treatments of the problem, the most famous of which is *Ludlul bel Nemeqi* ('I will praise the lord of wisdom'). A still earlier Sumerian treatment from the archives at Nippur has recently been discovered, though it is fragmentary and as yet unpublished.

The book of Ecclesiastes is probably to be dated by language and content in the 3rd century B.C., but so far no real archaeological parallel to it has been discovered. Skeptical poems of an earlier date are known from Egypt and Mesopotamia, but the temper of Ecclesiastes may have been influenced by a Greek atmosphere of thought in the Near Eastern world.

The Song of Songs is a collection of love lyrics probably edited in the Persian period, judging from the presence within it of certain Persian words. The songs themselves, however, are much older than this and were probably derived from Egyptian and Canaanite lyrics. The closest parallels are from Egypt, dating from the period 1300–1000 B.C. There, as in the biblical book, the songs are alternately placed in the mouths of the lover and the beloved, who address each other as 'brother' and 'sister'. The geographical allusions in the Song, however, indicate that its authors are Israelite. The archaeological discoveries in Egypt have simply revealed the existence of a type of ancient literature to which the Israelite book is related.

While the purpose and date of Daniel have long been established, the date and original character of Esther remain without archaeological confirmation. In type the book resembles the apocryphal stories of Tobit and Judith from the 3rd and 2nd centuries B.C., though it may belong to a slightly earlier period around 300 B.C.

A discussion of the role of archaeology in illuminating the history of the Hebrew language and of the script in which it was written would be too technical to include here. Before 1925 the student of Hebrew was generally trained in classical Arabic as the most important cognate language. While Arabic is still very important for vocabulary and verbal system, today the student receives a far more basic training in North-west Semitic, because it is now possible to reconstruct the earlier stages of the Hebrew language from contemporary sources. This is done through the study of Hebrew, Aramaic, and Phoenician inscriptions, and particularly through the study of Ugaritic, the language of the Canaanite religious documents found at Ras Shamra. The evolution of the Hebrew script can now be traced with considerable accuracy from about 1500 B.C. to modern times. Thus an expert can now give approximate dates to documents on the basis of the way in which the letters are formed.

The Discovery of Old Testament Manuscripts

The Hebrew manuscript used by most scholars today, when they read the Old Testament in its original language, dates from the 10th century A.D. Two portions of the Hebrew Bible, one in London and the other in Cairo, date from the preceding century. The oldest manuscript in the possession of the Samaritan sect at Nablus in Palestine dates from A.D. 655–56. Before 1947 these were the oldest manuscripts of the Old Testament in Hebrew that were known, except for the Nash Papyrus. This is a single leaf found in Egypt, dating from about 100 B.C. It contains the Ten Commandments and the *Shema* (Deut. 6. 4–5) and was never a part of a longer scroll but was a separate sheet used in teaching or worship.

Since the mediaeval Hebrew manuscripts represent only one textual tradition, textual criticism of the Old Testament has only been possible with the aid of translations, particularly the Septuagint. Codex Vaticanus and Codex Sinaiticus (4th century A.D.) are considerably older than the extant Hebrew manuscripts, and there are also portions of the Old Testament in Greek among the biblical papyri (2nd or 3rd centuries A.D.) found in Egypt. Two small fragments of Deuteronomy in Greek from about 100 B.C. have been published.

Nevertheless, it has been difficult to use the versions to correct the Hebrew, since we do not always know, where the Greek varies from the Hebrew, whether the Greek represents a different text or simply embodies a free translation.

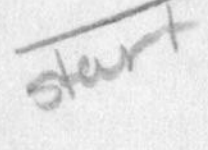

The discovery of the Dead Sea Scrolls, beginning in 1947, has radically altered the position in textual criticism. In the spring of 1947 an Arab shepherd accidentally discovered a number of parchment scrolls in a cave in the cliffs at the north-western edge of the Dead Sea. These scrolls subsequently came to the notice of the American School of Oriental Research and the Hebrew University of Jerusalem, and since then scholar and bedouin have been vying with each other in the search for more manuscripts, the bedouin having by far the greater success. Eleven caves in the Qumran area have so far yielded important material, the largest group of manuscript fragments being that discovered in Cave 4 in 1952. The discoveries are the fragmentary remains of the library of the Essenes, a Jewish sect which retired to the area presumably during the 2nd century B.C. and was forced to leave when the Romans besieged and destroyed their center about A.D. 68. Their beliefs and practices, and their probable influence on the New Testament, will be discussed in the next chapter. Here it is sufficient to note that the remains of their library must all be dated before A.D. 68. Other caves in the Wadi Murabba'at, south of Qumran, have yielded manuscripts of a slightly later date, mostly from the time of the Second Jewish Revolt in A.D. 132–35.

Most of the fragments are from a large number of non-biblical works, some already known, but most hitherto unknown. The commentaries on Isaiah, the Psalms, and some of the minor prophets are evidence of an intense study of the Scriptures, which also inspired the composition of a great variety of theological and apocalyptic works.

The biblical manuscripts can be identified quickly by the careful book-hand in which they were written and by the fine quality and color of the parchment used. Every book of the Old Testament is represented, except Esther. The most popular were Deuteronomy, Isaiah, and the Psalms, ten or more copies of each having been identified. It has been possible to arrange the fragments in the approximate order in which they were written on palaeographical evidence, i.e., by studying the evolution of the script. The staff of experts now studying the fragments believe that fragments of a scroll of Samuel (4QSam[b]) and of one of Jeremiah (4QJer[a]) are to be dated not far from 200 B.C., and may have belonged to the original library brought to Qumran by the Essenes. Fragments of Ecclesiastes come from the middle of the 2nd century B.C.: the fact that these are written in the book-hand and on the parchment used for other biblical books suggests that the date (*c.* 200 B.C.) assigned by some to Ecclesiastes in the past is too late. The complete Isaiah scroll (1QIsa[a]) is to be dated about 100 B.C., and the other Isaiah manuscript (1QIsa[b]) was copied in the late 1st century B.C.; this again suggests that Isaiah reached its present form long before the 2nd century. This argument does not apply, however, to the book of Daniel: the existence of three copies, one of them (from 1Q) from the early 1st century B.C., and therefore within a century of the composition of the book, suggests rather the importance attached to it by the sect. Only in the case of the Rylands fragment of the Gospel of John do we possess a biblical manuscript so near to the date of composition.

The importance of the fragments from Cave 4 is that they permit a sampling of the text of all the biblical books. While most of the fragments show little significant variation from the received Hebrew text, some are strikingly similar to the Septuagint, proving that the Greek translation does indeed rest on a Hebrew text tradition known and used in Palestine during and before the time of Christ. For example, one of the most important scrolls is a copy of 1 and 2 Samuel made about the time Jesus was born (4QSam[a]), in which portions of most chapters are preserved. Now it has long been recognized that the Hebrew text of Samuel is unusually corrupt, while in many places the Greek translation makes much better sense. The Qumran scroll in question is very close to the Greek, and even when it varies from it sometimes represents a better text. In fact, if the complete scroll had been preserved it would probably have been the most reliable copy of Samuel available. As it is, the fragments we still have make it possible to correct the received Hebrew text in a great number of places with far more confidence than before.

The Qumran discoveries, therefore, are of extraordinary importance, for they enable the scholar to get behind the standardized Hebrew text into a period when the transmission of the text was more fluid and when variant traditions had not yet been eliminated.

Maps, Texts, and Illustrations

Maps

WHA, Plates VIID, XIC, D, XIIA, XVIIB, XVIII; Grollenberg, Maps 21–31

Texts

(p. 129) The Cyrus Cylinder: *ANE*, 206–8; *ANET*, 315–16; *DOTT*, 92–4

(p. 132) The Elephantine Papyri: *ANE*, 278–82; *ANET*, 491–2; *DOTT*, 256–69

(p. 132) The Murashu Archives: *ANET*, 221–2; *DOTT*, 95–6

(p. 140) The Wisdom of Amen-em-opet: *ANE*, 237–43; *ANET*, 421–25

(p. 140) *Ludlul bel Nemeqi*: *ANET*, 434–7

(p. 140) Egyptian Love Songs: *ANE*, 257–8; *ANET*, 467–9; *DOTT*, 187–91

Illustrations (The references are to Figures)

(p. 129) The Cyrus Cylinder: *DOTT*, 6; Wiseman, 70

(p. 131) Seal impressions: Wright, 145

(p. 132) *Yehud* coins: *DOTT*, 14 (and pp. 233–4)

(p. 132) The Elephantine Papyri: *ANEP*, 282; Grollenberg, 261–4; *DOTT*, 16; Wright, 151

(p. 137) Marisa: Wright, 152
(p. 137) Hellenistic Samaria: *ANE*, 178; *ANEP*, 720; Wright, 153
(p. 140) The Wisdom of Amen-em-opet: *DOTT*, 9
(p. 142) The Dead Sea Scrolls: *ANE*, 83; *ANEP*, 284; Grollenberg, 346; Wiseman, 74–5; Wright, 155–9

CHAPTER IX

PALESTINE IN THE TIME OF CHRIST

AFTER the Romans took control of Palestine in 63 B.C., the country never again attained independent status in ancient times. When the Parthians of Mesopotamia threatened to take over Jerusalem in 40 B.C., the Romans gave most of the country into the hands of a man named Herod, who ruled as a client-king from 37 to 4 B.C. Herod was of Idumaean (Edomite) ancestry, but formally a Jew because his people were forcibly 'converted' by John Hyrcanus in 125 B.C. Actually, however, he was a great believer in Greek culture, and his reign is marked by the complete victory of Hellenism over the more conservative tendencies of the Maccabees.

PALESTINE AT THE TIME OF JESUS' BIRTH

Herod carried out a remarkable building campaign in the western tradition throughout his realm. According to the historian Josephus, 'there was not any place of his kingdom fit for the purpose that was permitted to be without somewhat that was for Caesar's honor'.[1] Let us examine the evidence from three cities in particular.

Samaria was completely changed. During the Maccabaean wars it had lost its fortification walls. These had been replaced between 57 and 55 B.C., but the city was far from attaining its former glory. However, in 37 B.C. Herod

[1] *Wars of the Jews*, Book I, Chapter XXI.

married his beloved Mariamne there, and seven years later the city was formally given him by Caesar Augustus. He settled 6,000 of his war veterans there, renamed the city Sebaste (Augusta), and fortified it with the double purpose of strengthening his hold upon the country and at the same time publicizing his gratitude and devotion to Augustus.

Herod's new city wall along the lower slopes of the mound enclosed a very large area, one kilometer in width at its greatest extent. The fortification was adequate, though not exceptional. The major effort was expended on the erection of a magnificent temple in honor of Augustus. Apart from the temple, the finest remaining ruin of the Herodian period is a stadium, built at the edge of the valley north of the mound, but purposely enclosed within the fortification walls. It was the regulation Olympic length (600 feet); a stadium at Miletus in Asia Minor is precisely the same length, though only half as wide. The stadium at Samaria was used for centuries, and indeed was completely rebuilt in Corinthian style about A.D. 200. It is not mentioned in ancient literature as the place where any famous contests were held, though we know that Herod was a great lover of athletic games, founding them at Caesarea and Jerusalem. At Caesarea, Josephus tells us, Herod arranged for games to be held every 5th year, and he is said to have endowed the whole Olympiad institution when it faltered for lack of money.

The second city to be mentioned is Caesarea, midway along the coast between Mt. Carmel and Joppa. Before Herod's day it was an unimportant site called 'Straton's Tower'. After the king had finished with it, the city was one of the most beautiful and important in Palestine. For most of the period A.D. 6–66 it was the seat of the Roman government in the country. Paul was tried there (Acts 25.

23 ff.). In the 2nd century of our era the city became an important center of the Christian Church.

Caesarea has never really been excavated, but the remains of the Roman city can still be seen. Herod spent twelve years (25–13 B.C.) in building it. A sea mole was built to make a harbor the equal of that at Athens. A semicircular wall was erected to enclose the main part of the city with its great public buildings. These included a temple in Caesar's honor, adorned with a colossal statue of him, an amphitheater, a theater, a stadium, and a marketplace. The ruins of the theater, amphitheater, and stadium are still visible; the amphitheater has only recently been discovered by Israeli archaeologists with the aid of an aerial photograph. This was the place where gladiators fought with each other and with wild beasts when the town was publicly inaugurated by Herod in 10 B.C., and where hundreds of Jewish prisoners were killed in such combats by Titus in A.D. 70.

The third city to be described as an example of Herod's transformation of Palestine is Jerusalem. There, among other things, he repaired the city fortifications, built a new temple for the Jews, rebuilt a citadel at the north-west corner of the temple area and called it 'The Tower of Antonia', and built a magnificent palace for himself.

By the time of Jesus the central part of the city was no longer on the lower hill (Ophel), south of the Temple area, where it had been in Old Testament times. It was now to the west and north of the sacred precincts. Furthermore, the Tyropoeon valley, which used to separate the eastern section of the city from the western, was now partially filled up with the debris of the centuries. During the Maccabaean age the Jews had erected a strong fortress on the site of the old city, which in Herod's day was called the

Acra. Josephus tells us that the old city was once higher than the temple area, but that when the Maccabees built the Acra they cut down the hill's height and filled in the valley between it and the Temple.

The problem of defense in New Testament times was not the same as in the time of David. Then the tremendous Canaanite fortifications of the lower hill had simply to be repaired. By New Testament times the main problem was the protection of both the eastern and the western hills, together with the rapidly expanding suburbs to the north. The southern and eastern boundaries had a natural protection in the deep valleys of the Hinnom and Kidron respectively, and could be easily fortified. On the north there were two walls. The first extended westward from about the middle of the Temple enclosure. The second began in the region of the north-western corner of the Temple area and evidently met the first at or near the present Jaffa Gate and the citadel, though its exact line is uncertain. If the Church of the Holy Sepulcher marks the spot of Jesus' crucifixion and burial, then the line of the second wall must be drawn in such a way as to leave this church outside it. Since this makes a rather unsatisfactory line for a fortification, some scholars believe that this church does not mark the historical place of Jesus' death and that the second wall enclosed a larger area, having been built on higher ground. About A.D. 42, in the reign of Herod Agrippa, a third wall was begun still farther north to enclose another suburb which Josephus calls Bezetha. It was not completed, however, until the period of the First Jewish Revolt against Rome in A.D. 66.

The first and second walls were already in existence when Herod became king. He strengthened them, especially by erecting three large towers at the place where they joined together, thus protecting the fortifications at their weakest point. Directly south of them he erected his sumptuous palace. At the place where the second wall approached the Temple enclosure he rebuilt a Maccabaean fortress and named it Antonia in honor of Mark Antony. Josephus tells us that the castle of Antonia stood on a precipice nearly 75 feet high, and that it had towers at its four corners, the one at the south-east being high enough for all that went on in the Temple area to be clearly visible. A Roman legion was quartered in the Antonia.

Jerusalem has been carefully studied and repeatedly excavated in modern times. Most of the excavations, however, were carried out before 1930, and careful stratigraphical techniques combined with a detailed study of pottery fragments were seldom used. The result is that while important discoveries have been made, most of them cannot be dated. Perhaps the finest work from a scientific viewpoint has been that of C. N. Johns (1934–40) in the citadel at the Jaffa Gate. It is at this spot that the first and second walls met and were strengthened by the three Herodian towers. Mr. Johns found beneath the courtyard of the citadel a pre-Herodian wall of the 3rd or 2nd century B.C., curving southward and strengthened by three towers. The foundations of one of the latter are still used to support the present 'Tower of David'; this tower at least was one of the three erected by Herod.

The situation and approximate plan of the Antonia have been fixed by the investigations of the French archaeologist Father H. Vincent. This was the place where Paul was imprisoned when a Roman officer rescued him from a mob in the Temple (Acts 21. 27 ff.), and in Father Vincent's view it was also the place where Jesus was tried before Pilate (Mark 15). The ancient street level in this area is some $6\frac{1}{2}$ feet below the present surface. Practically the only remnant of ancient construction still existing above ground is the Ecce Homo Arch, so called because tradition has claimed it as the place where Pilate showed Jesus to the mob and said: 'Behold the man!' (John 19. 5). Actually, however, this arch never had a connection with the Tower of Antonia or with the life of Jesus. It was once a triple arch and was erected by the Roman emperor Hadrian (A.D. 117–38), as the triumphal entry-way into the new city which he had built and from which all Jews were excluded.

The most impressive discovery made by Father Vincent was the pavement that once covered the floor of the Antonia. It is probably the pavement mentioned in John 19. 13. Scratched on the stone slabs was a pattern for a popular Roman game evidently played by the soldiers stationed there.

The finest remains of Herodian construction in Jerusalem are those of the special wall built around the great court occupied by the Temple. This enclosed a much larger courtyard than hitherto because the Jerusalem sanctuary was now a place of pilgrimage for Jews from all over the civilized world. To provide a courtyard of sufficient size it was necessary to build a platform supported by columns and immense vaults over a portion of the south-eastern area where the ground fell rapidly away. These vaults are still there, and are called 'Solomon's Stables', because tradition has attributed them to Solomon. The Crusaders are said to have stabled their horses there, and this may explain why they are called stables.

To support the platform Herod further built a massive retaining wall around it, portions of which are still to be seen on the western, southern, and south-eastern sides of the enclosure. The 'Wailing Wall' on the west is the most vivid example, the lower courses being characteristic of Herod's workmanship.

Descriptions of Herod's Temple have been preserved in Josephus and in the Mishnah (Tractate Middoth). It was evidently a magnificent structure, worthy of comparison with the great temples of the Roman world. It was looted and burned in A.D. 70, when the soldiers of Titus laid waste the whole city (cf. Mk. 13. 2). Only two pieces of stone have been found which are known to have belonged to it. They were once set in the gates leading to the Temple's inner court, and they bear a notice in Greek which reads: 'No alien may enter within the barrier and wall around the Temple. Whoever is caught (violating this) is alone responsible for the death(-penalty) which follows.'

The general plan of the Temple was fixed by tradition and the existing sanctuary. All Herod could do was to make it higher, affix a magnificent portico, and decorate it elaborately, gold plates over the front being an example. Around it were cloistered courts with beautiful colonnades. A defective column which was intended for use in the cloisters but never moved from the quarry was discovered years ago in front of the Russian cathedral north of the old city. The cloisters were not completed in Herod's day: they were finished only six years before the whole was destroyed in A.D. 70.

The Essenes

The chief Jewish sects in Palestine during the time of Jesus were the Sadducees, the Pharisees, and the Essenes. The Sadducees were aristocratic and theologically conservative priests who denied any doctrine which they could not find in the Scriptures, particularly the comparatively new doctrines of the resurrection of the dead and of future punishment in hell. The Pharisees were the theologians and strict legalists of the day, who accepted the developed doctrines of heaven and hell, resurrection and immortality, but who also laid great emphasis on a large body of oral interpretations of the Law of Moses and considered them of binding authority. Both of these groups were severely castigated in the New Testament, but no mention is made of the third group, the Essenes. We read about them in Josephus, who says that they held their property in common, followed a fairly ascetic discipline, held to a lofty moral code which was 'better than that of other men', and did not offer sacrifices in the Temple 'because they have more pure lustrations of their own'.[1] Pliny the elder also mentions them: he says that they lived on the west side of the Dead Sea, 'a solitary race, and strange above all others in the entire world'.[2]

Pliny's statement that the Essenes (or at least their main colony) lived near the Dead Sea has helped to identify them with the group which owned the Dead Sea or Qumran scrolls. Among the scrolls are documents, particularly a Manual of Discipline, which tell us far more about the sect than we had hitherto known. In addition, the community center at Khirbet Qumran has been excavated. A large compound was erected there on the site of a Judaean fortress. It was begun in the late 2nd century B.C., suffered badly in an earthquake in 31 B.C., but was repaired and used again until destroyed in A.D. 68 by the Tenth Roman Legion. Thereafter only a military fort existed at the site until the end of the 1st century A.D. The discovery of a scriptorium shows that in the community center the

[1] *Antiquities of the Jews*, Book XVIII, Chapter I; see also *Wars of the Jews*, Book II, Chapter VIII.
[2] *Natural History*, V. 17.

Essenes studied the Scriptures and copied scrolls for the library. Here, too, they ate their common meals and worshipped together, though their living quarters were probably in the caves of the neighboring cliffs.

From the documents we gather that the sect was founded in Maccabaean times by the 'Teacher of Righteousness'. The group went into the wilderness 'to prepare there the way of the Lord', regarding themselves as a community set apart, 'being united (so as to constitute) a holy of holies and a house of community for the Israel(ites) who walk in perfection'.[1]

Like the disciples of John the Baptist and Jesus, this group was an eschatological community, which accepted a special discipline and task in preparation for the end-time in which God's kingdom would be established under the leadership of the Messiah. They revived the old Israelite conception of the Holy War, preserved particularly in Deuteronomy, and organized themselves into a little 'salvation-army', giving themselves wholly to a rigorous discipline and organization. Like the New Testament community, they appear to have had twelve of their number as their chosen leaders, perhaps as a symbol of the twelve Israelite tribes.[2] All property was held in common (cf. Acts 4. 32–37), and the center of their life was the joint study of the Scriptures and the sacrament of a common banquet, at which a priest stretched forth 'his hand to invoke a blessing with the first of the bread and wine'.

Entrance into the group meant renouncing one's former ties and undergoing a period of training. The initiatory rite was baptism, but this was repeated at intervals as a sign of

[1] *The Dead Sea Manual of Discipline*, tr. by W. H. Brownlee, *BASOR Supplementary Studies*, Nos. 10–12 (1951), Section viii, 13–14; ix, 6.

[2] Interpreting 'twelve laymen and three priests' (*Manual of Discipline*, viii, 1) as meaning twelve men, three of whom are priests.

purification from evil thoughts and intentions, on which great stress was laid. Repeated examinations before one's elders were held. The procedure of neighborly reproof seems to have been precisely the same as that given by Jesus in Matt. 18. 15–17.[1] The Essenes thought of themselves as following 'the Way' (cf. Acts 9. 2), and one of the names for the community was 'the Many', which lay behind the 'multitude' of Acts 4. 32; 6. 2, 5; 15. 12, 30. Thus there are a number of similarities between the Essene community and the early Jerusalem church.

The early Church understood that many passages of the Old Testament were fulfilled in the recent great events by which it had been founded. This method of interpreting Scripture is not rabbinic, but it is paralleled in the biblical commentaries of the Essenes, where events in the history of the sect are found foretold in the Old Testament. They even possessed lists of proof-texts relating to the Messiah similar to that which it is believed the author of the Gospel of Matthew must have possessed.

The Essenes seem to have been influenced by Iranian or Zoroastrian religious thinking, since for them the world is the scene of a conflict between the forces of good and evil, light and darkness, truth and falsehood.[2] The same type of ethical dualism is found throughout the New Testament, particularly in Paul (Eph. 2. 2; 3. 10) and in John. 1 John 4. 6 appears to refer directly to the Essene doctrine of the two spirits of truth and falsehood, and the 'Spirit of truth' (John 14. 17; 15. 26; 16. 13) is similarly reminiscent, especially as 'truth' in John is something to be done (3. 21). John also makes frequent use of the opposition between

[1] *Manual of Discipline*, v. 25–vi. 1.

[2] The Essau creed is summarized in the *Manual of Discipline*, iii. 13–iv. 26.

light and darkness. Thus part at least of the background of John's thinking may be found in the Essene theology of Palestine.

The differences between the Essene and Christian movements are, however, still more impressive than the similarities. The Qumran sect were conservative legalists who sought salvation in the Mosaic Law, as a preparation for the coming of the Messiah and his kingdom. The Christian Gospel could not be contained in the 'old wineskins' of the Mosaic Law. Christ's saving work was for all sinners, not simply for a few elect followers. The Essene Gospel of the new righteousness in the New Covenant is far removed from the Christian Gospel of God's love, just as the figure of Christ is very different from the Essene 'Teacher of Righteousness'.

Archaeology and the Gospels

The period covered by New Testament history is so short that archaeology cannot be expected to be as helpful as it has been with Old Testament history, which covers a period of 1,500 years. Some idea of the cultural background to the ministry of Jesus has been given. A few illustrations of the light shed on various historical and geographical details in the Gospel record may also be mentioned.

The Gospel of Luke tells us that Jesus was born in Bethlehem because Joseph and Mary had to go there to be enrolled for taxation. This enrollment was ordered by Caesar Augustus (27 B.C.–A.D. 14) when Quirinius was governor of Syria, and it is said to have been the first such taxation-census (Luke 2. 1–3). We have a number of witnesses to this type of census during the Roman period, and the evidence suggests that the practice began during the reign of Caesar Augustus. Furthermore, an Egyptian papyrus indicates that in A.D. 103–4 there was a census in Egypt which was made on the basis of kinship, and proclamation was then made for all who were residing elsewhere to return to their family home.

We also have information about Sulpicius Quirinius. He was a Roman senator who was first sent out from Rome to quell a disturbance in Asia Minor in 10–7 B.C. He was Roman governor in A.D. 6–9, during which time a census was taken, which resulted in a serious Jewish rebellion in Galilee. Yet this census was too late to have occurred at the time of Jesus' birth, since he was born before the death of Herod the Great in 4 B.C. (Luke 1. 5; Mt. 2. 1). Quirinius may have been governor in 3–2 B.C. as well, but that date too is after the death of Herod. This chronological problem has not been solved.

Jesus' ministry took place during the reign of Tiberius (A.D. 14–37), when Pontius Pilate was the governor or procurator of Judaea (A.D. 26–36), Herod Antipas the tetrarch of Galilee and part of Transjordan (4 B.C.–A.D. 39), and his brother Philip the tetrarch of the area north and east of the Sea of Galilee (4 B.C.–A.D. 34). This information is accurately given us in Luke 3. 1. The Romans had taken over the administration of the province of Judaea, but had left other areas in the hands of local rulers. This meant that the areas in which the ministry of Jesus took place were under the control of different rulers. Yet it seems that Jesus was able to move freely, not only in Galilee, but also in the territory of Philip (Mark 8. 27), the Decapolis,[1] the

[1] A group of Hellenistic cities in Transjordan, originally ten in number, which had been in existence since the 3rd or 2nd century B.C. and had been banded together by the Romans under the separate political control of the governor of Syria. The best known were Gerasa (modern Jerash) and Philadelphia (modern Amman). The former has been called 'the Pompeii of Palestine', but most of its monuments are later than the 1st century A.D.

Palestinian portions of the province of Syria (Mark 7. 24, 31), and Judaea. By the middle of the 2nd century A.D. the various military camps in those areas were connected with each other and with the outside world by a magnificent series of Roman roads, but none of these had been built in the time of Jesus.

The main cities and towns mentioned in the Gospel narratives have long been known. The location of Capernaum, however, has not been finally settled. Most geographers from the 17th to the 19th century used to locate it at a ruin called Khan Minyeh on the north-western shore of the Sea of Galilee. In 1905, however, excavations were begun at a site farther north, called Tell Hum. The remains of a fine synagogue were unearthed and partly restored, and this site is now generally taken to agree better with ancient testimony regarding Capernaum than Khan Minyeh. The synagogue at Tell Hum is often pointed out as the one in which Jesus worshipped. Unfortunately archaeologists now believe that it must be dated about A.D. 200, long after the time of Jesus. Earlier ruins of the 1st century A.D. may be beneath it or elsewhere in the site, but further excavation is needed before we can be sure.

Other synagogues in Galilee besides the one at Capernaum were once thought to go back to the time of Christ. Modern study, however, has shown that no surviving ruin of a synagogue is to be dated earlier than the end of the 2nd century A.D. The reason why no 1st century synagogues have been found in Palestine is that they were all destroyed in the Roman conquest of the Jews after their two revolts against Rome in A.D. 66–70 and 132–35. The archaeological discoveries indicate an almost complete disruption in the continuity of life as a result of the First Revolt.

The only certain fragment of a synagogue from before

A.D. 70 is an inscription found on Ophel, or the old lower city of Jerusalem, in 1913–14. Its text reads:

> Theodotus son of Vettenus, priest and synagogue-president, son of a synagogue-president and grandson of a synagogue-president, has built the synagogue for the reading of the Law and the teaching of the Commandments, and (he has built) the hostelry and the chambers and the cisterns of water in order to provide lodgings for those from abroad who need them—(the synagogue) which his fathers and the elders and Simonides had founded.

Theodotus' family name is thought to be derived from the Roman family of the Vetteni, which indicates that he or an ancestor was a Jewish freedman from Italy. Consequently the inscription is believed to refer to the 'Synagogue of the Freedmen' which is mentioned in Acts 6. 9. The members of this synagogue formed the strongest opposition to the preaching of Stephen, the first Christian martyr.

New Testament Manuscripts

The earliest manuscript of a New Testament book is a fragment of the Gospel of John in the John Rylands Library at Manchester, England, first published in 1935. It was found in Egypt and is dated in the early part of the 2nd century A.D. This proves that the Gospel was being circulated in Egypt less than fifty years after it was written. From approximately the same time there are larger fragments of a papyrus book of an 'Unknown Gospel'. The manuscript would appear to have been written by one who knew John and one or more of the Synoptics and also had access to material unknown to us.

The text of the New Testament is better attested by manuscript tradition than any other work from antiquity. The chief manuscripts are those of the 4th and 5th centuries which were added to the Septuagint, the Greek translation of the Old Testament. These are now supplemented by great numbers of other manuscripts and by 126 imperfect leaves of New Testament books among the Chester Beatty papyri, which are dated in the 3rd century. Among the latter is a codex of the letters of Paul, dating about A.D. 200, which is earlier by 150 years than the oldest copies of the Pauline letters otherwise known, and probably little more than a century from the time when the letters were collected and published together.

The codex is a book in the modern sense, with the leaves laid flat upon one another, in contrast to the scroll or roll. The latter was quite satisfactory for small documents, such as letters or for any literary work which is meant to be read through. Yet for a lengthy document to which constant reference needs to be made in order to look up specific passages, it was obviously less convenient than the leaf-book. The evidence now at hand suggests that Christians quickly began to use the codex almost exclusively for their works. During the 3rd century A.D., for example, nearly 85% of all Christian manuscripts discovered are of the codex type, while nearly 94% of the recovered non-Christian documents of the same period are still of the roll-type.

Perhaps the most unusual manuscript discoveries relating to the New Testament are the fragments of papyrus discovered at Oxyrhynchus in Egypt at the beginning of the present century. They contain a number of reputed sayings of Jesus and are probably to be dated in the 3rd and 4th centuries A.D. Most of the sayings are variants of some in the Gospels, but some are found nowhere else. For example:

> Jesus saith, 'Except ye keep (your life) in the world as a fast, ye shall not find the Kingdom of God; and except ye keep the (whole) week as a sabbath ye shall not see the Father.'
>
> Jesus saith, 'I stood in the midst of the world and in the flesh was I seen of them, and I found all men drunken, and none found I athirst among them; and my soul grieveth over the sons of men, because they are blind in their heart, and see not.'

These and other papyri are fragments of lost gospels and collections of the sayings of Jesus. While they whet our appetites for much more of the same, it is highly probable that the Early Church's special preservation of the four Gospels that we have was not purely accidental but a conscious selection of the most reliable material.

Maps, Texts, and Illustrations

Maps

WHA, Plates XIIB, XIII, XIV, XVIIC, XVIII; Grollenberg, Maps 32–5

Texts

(p. 154) The Dead Sea Scrolls: M. Burrows, *The Dead Sea Scrolls* (New York, 1955) and *More Light on the Dead Sea Scrolls* (New York, 1958); T. H. Gaster, *The Scriptures of the Dead Sea Sect* (London, 1956)

(p. 161) The Oxyrhynchus Papyri: M. R. James, *The Apocryphal New Testament* (Oxford, 1924), pp. 25–8

Illustrations (The references are to Figures)

(p. 147) Herod's Samaria: Grollenberg, 226, 228; Wright, 160
(p. 148) Caesarea: Grollenberg, 329–30; Wright, 161
(p. 151) The Tower of Antonia: Wright, 164
(p. 151) The Tower of David: Wright, 163
(p. 152) The Ecce Homo Arch: Wright, 165
(p. 152) Pavement of the Antonia: Wright, 166
(p. 152) The Wailing Wall: Grollenberg, 333; Wright, 167; *WHA*, 63; (5th ed.), 71
(p. 153) Herod's Temple: Wright, 168
(p. 153) The temple inscription: Wiseman, 101; Wright, 169
(p. 154) Qumran: Grollenberg, 347–50; Wright, 180–1; *WHA* (5th ed.), 60–1
(p. 158n.) Gerasa: Grollenberg, 296–9; Wright, 179; *WHA*, 41; (5th ed.), 45
(p. 158n.) Philadelphia: Grollenberg, 300–1
(p. 159) Synagogue at Capernaum: *ECW*, 35; Grollenberg, 365–7; Wright, 182; *WHA*, 37; (5th ed.), 41
(p. 160) The Theodotus Inscription: Wright, 183; *WHA*, 64; (5th ed.), 72
(p. 161) Codex Sinaiticus: Wiseman, 104
(p. 161) Chester Beatty Papyrus 11: Wright, 191

CHAPTER X

THE CHURCH IN THE WORLD

WITH the Acts of the Apostles and the Epistles the center of interest shifts from Palestine to a much wider world. After A.D. 70, when Jerusalem was destroyed, Christianity obtains its deepest rootage outside Palestine, and the Christian historian returns to Palestine only after the passage of many years, when Christian churches begin to be established there and the land becomes the 'Holy Land', a place of pilgrimage.

Initially, within the period covered by the New Testament, Christianity moved north and then west, drawn as by a magnet to Rome, the hub of the world at that time. The reason for this was the new unity imposed on the world by Roman power, Roman law, and Graeco-Roman culture. The Greek language, learned in Palestine by many of the earliest Christians, made it possible for them to be understood almost anywhere in the empire. Jewish communities were to be found in every major city, and to them the missionaries preached first. Roman provincial administration kept the roads safe and in good condition throughout the controlled areas. Only after Christianity was firmly entrenched in the Roman provinces of the east do we begin to encounter signs of its penetration into Mesopotamia and other areas independent of Rome.

EARLY CHRISTIAN CHURCHES IN THE EAST

The earliest evidence which the archaeologist has found for Christian communities in the east is in Egypt. The large number of papyrus fragments of the New Testament found in that country show that within 100 years of Jesus' death thriving Christian groups were in existence as far south as the Egyptian Fayum. The earliest remains of church architecture in Egypt, as in most other areas of the Roman Empire, are from the 4th century A.D., during and after the time of the emperor Constantine (A.D. 323–37), when Christianity became the official religion sponsored by the Roman government.

Many churches have been found in Palestine, and these too date after the time of Constantine, between the 4th and 6th centuries. The Church of the Holy Sepulcher in Jerusalem and the Church of the Nativity in Bethlehem were both built in Constantine's time, though little remains of the original structures within the later buildings now standing.

The oldest known church which archaeologists have found was that excavated in 1931–32 at Dura-Europos in eastern Syria on the Euphrates. This town was taken by the Romans and provided with a garrison in A.D. 167 as an outpost of the empire. South of the main gate was a church which had once been a private house. It consisted of a series of rooms around a paved open court. On a plastered wall was an inscription stating when the house was built, A.D. 232–33 in our calendar. One of the rooms had been used as a chapel, which was later enlarged by the opening of two more rooms so that the whole could seat about 100 people. In a small neighboring room was the baptistry, at one end of which was a receptacle for the water. Above this was painted on the wall a picture of Christ as the Good Shepherd—a very popular theme in early Christian art, as we know from painting and sculpture in Italy. Other wall paintings show scriptural scenes, such as David and Goliath, the Samaritan woman, Peter attempting to walk on the water, and the healing of the paralytic. The meeting-places of early Christians were in private houses for the most part, and the Dura building is an excellent example of one such house-church.

Elsewhere in Syria, and for that matter throughout the ancient world, virtually nothing remains of the churches which existed before the time of Constantine, though there are many Christian ruins which date from the 4th–6th centuries A.D. The reason probably is that most of the churches were destroyed in the violent persecutions of the emperor Diocletian, which began in A.D. 303. The archaeologist cannot hope to discover very much that directly illuminates the life of the Church during the second half of the 1st century A.D., when the number of Christians was comparatively small and scattered throughout a vast realm. All that we can do here, therefore, is to select some of the places which figure in Paul's missionary journeys in order to see how archaeology has illumined the geographic and cultural background against which the epistles of the New Testament were written.

Antioch in Syria

We begin with Antioch in Syria, which, after Rome and Alexandria, was the third city in the empire. It was the first major center of Christianity outside Palestine, and the base from which Paul set out on his missionary journeys. It was situated about 300 miles north of Jerusalem at the point where the Lebanon mountains and the Taurus range from Asia Minor meet. Antioch was founded about 300 B.C. on the banks of the Orontes some 20 miles from the sea. Through its seaport, Seleucia, it was in constant communication with the west, while trading caravans from all over the Near East converged upon it. During the 4th century A.D. its male citizens numbered 150,000–200,000, and we can assume at least the same number in Paul's day. It was the home of great philosophical, medical, and rhetorical schools, a famous library and all the public amusements in full measure: theaters, amphitheaters, stadia, and baths. Like other great Hellenistic cities, it was bisected from one end to the other by a great colonnaded street, but it is the only one known to us which had a regular system of street-lamps.

Near by at Daphne was a celebrated sanctuary of the god Apollo, which was notorious for vice. The citizens of Antioch also enjoyed a reputation for scurrilous wit and the invention of nicknames, of which the name 'Christian' (Acts 11. 26) may be an example. It was in this wildly pagan city that the Christian Church formed its great center outside Palestine. The physician Luke has traditionally been thought to be a native of this city, and the Gospel of Matthew may well have been written there.

Excavations were conducted in the city and its port Seleucia between 1931 and 1939. Perhaps the most important discoveries are hundreds of mosaic pavements which yield considerable information about the art and even the pagan religious cults of the later Roman and Byzantine periods. The remains of over a score of ancient churches have been identified in the city and its suburbs, all of them from the 4th century A.D. or later. Antioch once had a large Jewish colony, and associated with it was a large number of Greek converts or 'God-fearers'. It was probably from among the latter that the Christian Church received most of its initial converts. Yet with the possible exception of a 6th-century inscription which may contain a biblical phrase, the excavators have found no evidence of the Jewish community other than a marble fragment with a portion of a seven-branched candlestick upon it.

The best-known object from the area is 'The Chalice of Antioch'. Its discovery was announced in 1916. It is a plain silver cup surrounded by an outer shell decorated with vines and the figures of Christ and the apostles. The cup was claimed to be the Holy Grail, used by Jesus at the Last Supper, and the figures on the shell were interpreted as 1st century portraits. The work of a number of scholars, however, has virtually proved that it dates from about the 4th or 5th century A.D. and had nothing to do with the Last Supper. Nevertheless, it is still one of the most important pieces of early Christian silver in existence.

Galatia

On his first missionary journey Paul preached in Antioch of Pisidia, Iconium, Lystra, and Derbe (Acts 13. 14–14. 24) in the Roman province of Galatia. It was probably to the Christian communities there founded that Paul later wrote his Letter to the Galatians.

The name 'Galatia' was derived from a group of Gauls from Europe who settled in the northern part of the province during the 3rd century B.C. In the early 2nd century the area became a client-kingdom of Rome, was gradually enlarged, and after the death of its last king in 25 B.C. it became a Roman province. Antioch, the chief city of the province, was founded by Seleucus I of Syria about 300 B.C. as one of some sixteen Antiochs which he established and named after his father. About 189 B.C. it was made a free city by the Romans, and by 11 B.C. a Roman colony. As a free city, Antioch had an elective form of self-government, popular assemblies, and a system of education undoubtedly Hellenic in spirit. In such a city the political assembly was called by the Greek term *ekklesia*, which was the word the Christians borrowed for the Church. As a Roman colony, Antioch was placed in the highest rank of provincial cities, with a well-defined social stratification. At the top were the Latin-speaking Roman citizens (*coloni*), who had all the privileges in law of a citizen of Rome itself. The bulk of the populace, however, undoubtedly spoke Greek, and were ranked only as 'residents' (*incolae*) and lacked full civil rights.

Asia Minor was filled with a large variety of religious sects. Yet the old gods were faced with great difficulty in accommodating themselves to the new age. One of the great documents which circulated in Asia Minor, a partial duplicate of which was found in the excavations at Antioch, was the *Monumentum Ancyranum*, narrating the 'Deeds Accomplished by the Divine Augustus (Caesar)'. Another copy of this document was carved on the walls of the Augusteum, a white marble temple erected in Ancyra (Ankara) in northern Galatia. The text, which is probably by Augustus himself, was completed in A.D. 14. It described the emperor's life and work in the attempt to fulfil the religious, even Messianic, hopes of the time. By Paul's day these hopes had been dashed; the reign of the gods on earth had not come to pass. It is perhaps in this atmosphere that Paul preached in Antioch.

Excavations in Antioch just before and after the First World War uncovered some of the most important ruins of the Roman city of Paul's day. These included the Square of Augustus and the Square of Tiberius, connected by a stairway, at the top of which were triumphal archways erected in honor of Augustus. In the Square of Augustus was a great temple of the god Men, whose symbol was a bull's head. From a later period, the end of the 4th century A.D., came the ruins of a large Christian church. The city was evidently one of great architectural beauty and splendor, combining Greek refinement and simplicity with Roman complexity and massiveness.

Ephesus

On Paul's third missionary journey more than two years of his work centered in Ephesus. This was the chief city of the Roman province of Asia, with a population of at least a quarter of a million. Ephesus served as the connecting port for sea trade with the west and the land routes to the east. Literary and inscriptional evidence give eloquent testimony to the enormous wealth of the city. According to the Roman Strabo, it was the chief market of Asia Minor. No small part of its money and fame came from the cult of Artemis, the mother-goddess, whom the Romans identified with Diana. Her worship was connected with the fertility of the human family, flocks, and herds. Her background was Asiatic rather than Greek or Roman, and her worship was similar to that of the earlier fertility cults of Canaan, which were so seductive an influence upon Israel. The cult was popular, and the evidence supports the statement of Demetrius the silversmith that it was she 'whom all Asia and the world worshipped' (Acts 19. 27).

The temple of Artemis at Ephesus was considered one of the Seven Wonders of the ancient world. It was first systematically excavated by the English architect J. T. Wood, who discovered it after six years' work in 1869. Its first primitive structures, dating back to the 8th century

B.C., were little more than an enclosure containing a platform, a sacred tree and altar, and perhaps later a wooden image. About 550 B.C. the temple was constructed on a much grander scale. This survived according to tradition until it was burned in 356 B.C. It was succeeded by what is known as the Hellenistic temple, begun in 350 B.C. and completed at the expense of Alexander the Great. This temple stood until A.D. 262, when it was sacked by the Goths. Behind it stood the statue of the goddess which is said to have 'fallen from Jupiter' (Acts 19. 35): that is, it may have been sculptured from a large meteorite. White marble tiles covered the roof, and the building was adorned with sculpture, excellent painting, and gold.

The month of Artemision (March–April) was a time when tourists and religious enthusiasts must have brought great wealth to the temple and the tradesmen. Perhaps it was these crowds that kept Paul in Ephesus until after Pentecost (1 Cor. 16. 8–9). This was a likely time for the riots occasioned by the economic results of his preaching and by jealousy for the gods. The mob, stirred up by Demetrius the silversmith, whose name may possibly have been found on an inscription, gathered against Paul in the great theater on the western slope of Mt. Pion overlooking the city. This theater is said to have accommodated 24,550 persons.

Perhaps the most important work at the site has been that of the Austrian Archaeological Institute, which began its excavations in 1896. Practically all the main buildings of the ancient city have been unearthed. The market-place (Greek *agora*, Latin *forum*) was a large open square, surrounded by colonnades and various important buildings. Most impressive is the 'Arkadiane', the street which ran from the theater to the harbor, over a quarter of a mile long. It was paved in marble, was 36 feet wide, and was lined by a colonnade behind which were shops.

Numerous inscriptions found in the city contain information of importance to the Christian archaeologist. The mention of exorcists in Acts 19. 13 recalls the popularity of specialists in magical formulas and incantations, which Greek and Roman writers refer to as 'Ephesian writings'. The formula 'I adjure you by . . .', used by patronizing Jewish magicians in Acts 19. 13, appears to have been the regular formula of exorcism. The word in Acts 19. 18 which the Authorized Version translates 'deeds' really means here 'magical formulas'. The 'Asiarchs' of Acts 19. 31 are frequently mentioned in the Ephesian inscriptions: it was a title for a leader in the rites of the emperor-cult in the province of Asia. Acts 19. 35 mentions the 'town clerk', who from the inscriptions was evidently the leading public official of the city. The same verse mentions Ephesus as the 'temple keeper' of Artemis, and one of the inscriptions says the same thing. This title was also used at Ephesus and elsewhere, however, to indicate that the city was 'temple keeper' for the worship of the Roman emperor.

The First Churches in Europe

On his second missionary journey Paul crossed from Asia Minor into Europe, and made his way inland to the city of Philippi. The chief monuments of Philippi were excavated by the École Française d'Athènes between 1914 and 1938.

The Egnatian Way, a paved Roman road across Macedonia to the Adriatic, was once the main thoroughfare of Philippi, and in places the ruts worn in the stone by countless wagons and chariots can still be seen. On the western side of the city a great arched gateway was uncovered; through it the road passed and about a mile from the city crossed a small river. This is the only possible place in the neighborhood to which Acts 16. 13 could refer: 'On the sabbath day we went outside the gate to the riverside, where we supposed there was a place of prayer.' Evidently the Jewish community in the city was too small to have a synagogue. Inside the gates the Roman forum has been uncovered, and though the present remains represent a rebuilding of the 2nd century A.D., they probably illustrate the general plan as it was when Paul was there. On the north side of the forum was a podium with steps leading up the two sides. This was the tribunal for orators and magistrates, and undoubtedly marks the spot to which Paul and Silas were dragged and where they were sentenced to prison (Acts 16. 19 ff.). An ancient writer says that the prison was among the other buildings which bordered the forum, but its exact location has not been fixed.

The plain of Philippi was the scene of the great battle for the control of the Roman empire after the death of Julius Caesar in 42 B.C. To celebrate the victory Antony and Octavian made the city a Roman colony, and veterans of the battle were among its first citizens (*coloni*). The arched gateway and the enlargement of the city from a small town around its acropolis probably date from this time.

The next major city along the Via Egnatia in which Paul founded a church was Thessalonica, about 70 miles from Philippi. It is the modern Salonica, the largest city of Greece after Athens. No major excavations have been attempted there because of the modern buildings. The city was founded about 315 B.C. and named after the sister of

Alexander the Great. The Egnatian Way is still its main thoroughfare, and at one point it is spanned by a fine triple arch erected by the emperor Galerius (A.D. 305–11). The western entrance to the city was once covered by another Roman arch, called the Varder Gate, which remained standing until 1876, when it was removed for modern construction. An inscription on this gate, now in the British Museum, mentions some city officials called 'politarchs'. A number of other inscriptions contain the same word. In Acts 17. 6 this is also used as the title of the officials before whom the Christians were dragged during the riot caused by Paul's preaching. The word is otherwise unknown in extant Greek literature, and the archaeological information is a confirmation of the accuracy of Luke's narrative at this point.

Athens

After leaving the Macedonian cities of Thessalonica and Beroea, Paul went to Athens. Athens was now well past the height of its golden age, which flowered in the 5th century B.C., but it was still one of the world's leading centers for philosophy, architecture, poetry, and art. In it there still remain today some of the most remarkable and best preserved of the monuments of antiquity.

The ancient center of the city, the agora or market-place, is not only being excavated; it is also being restored. It was in this agora and in the synagogue that Paul argued daily with the Jews, devout persons, and those 'that chanced to be there' (Acts 17. 17). The agora was the political, commercial, and social center of the ancient Greek town, and consisted of a large open space bordered by public, religious, and political buildings.

Most of the majestic architecture of the Acropolis to the

south dates to the golden age of Pericles, the 5th century B.C. Crowning the hill is the extraordinary Parthenon, within which Phidias, Pericles' sculptor, erected a gold-and-ivory statue of Athena. According to Pausanias, a traveler who visited Athens between A.D. 143 and 159, a colossal bronze statue of the Athena Promachos towered above the Acropolis, and mariners could see the sunlight flashing on her helmet and spear.[1]

As the New Testament student reads about Paul's short stay in Athens the incident that most claims his interest is the speech on the Areopagus (Acts 17. 19–31). This rocky bare hill a little north-west of the Acropolis was the meeting-place of the Athenian Court for religious and political matters. In the time of Pericles it had been mainly a criminal court, but by Roman times it was again concerned with religion and education. The place of the Court's assembly was also called the Areopagus, so that we are uncertain whether Acts is referring to the hill or to the Court.

The other problem Paul's speech presents is his quotation of the inscription 'To an unknown god'. No such inscription has yet been found in Athens. The traveler Pausanias and some later literary works, however, speak of 'unknown gods', and an altar 'to unknown gods' was discovered at Pergamum in Asia. Hence there is nothing really strange about the reference which Paul makes.

Corinth

From Athens Paul went to Corinth, where he stayed a year and six months. Corinth commanded the land route over the narrow isthmus connecting central Greece and the Peloponnesus; it was thus a natural center for the sea

[1] *Description of Greece*, I. xxviii. 2.

trade of Lechaion on the west and Cenchreae on the east. Small ships were dragged the short distance between the two cities and other cargo was taken overland and re-loaded. Otherwise the ships had to make the dangerous 200-mile trip around the peninsula. The Corinth canal that was cut across the narrowest point of the isthmus between 1881 and 1893 follows practically the same route as that planned and begun by Nero in A.D. 66. Located in such a situation, Corinth was a great commercial center, and Caesar Augustus made it the capital of the Roman province of Achaia and seat of its proconsul.

Excavation has been possible only because in 1858 an earthquake caused old Corinth to be abandoned. The earliest occupation of the site goes back to the 4th millennium B.C., and its history shows various invasions, destructions, and subsequent returns to glory. In 146 B.C. it was destroyed by the Romans, but probably not as completely as was formerly thought. After the site had lain idle for a century a Roman colony was planted, and the city was again on its way to prosperity. In Paul's day it was in the midst of reconstruction and expansion.

In the center of the city was the agora or market-place, where the important civic and religious buildings were situated. The Lechaion Road led into the agora from the north, and various constructions partially preserved reveal shops opening on the street or courtyard, doubtless similar to the one in which Paul worked at his trade with Priscilla and Aquila (Acts 18. 2–3). On the right, just before the road entered the agora, there was a large columned hall or basilica. This type of building was used by Romans for civic and judicial purposes, and from it Christians later derived their plan for the nave and aisle type of church. To the left was the Peribolos of Apollo, one of several sanctuaries to this god, and the fountain house of Periene, Corinth's most important reservoir and still a source of water today. The Propylaea by which one entered the agora consisted of a broad stairway which was once surmounted by a monumental gateway. At the foot of these stairs an inscription was found which read 'Synagogue of the Jews'. Though later than the time of Paul, it may indicate that the synagogue in which Paul preached was not far from this area.

In the agora basilicas, temples, and stoas with shops lined the sides. In one of these shops a stone block was found which was originally a doorstep; it bears an inscription which reads: 'Lucius the butcher'. This may indicate the section of shops which was the Corinthian meat market mentioned by Paul in 1 Cor. 10. 25.

The large and unencumbered open space of the agora was divided into two levels. The well-built and elaborate Rostra of the higher level was probably the platform to which Paul was taken before Gallio (Acts 18. 12–17). An inscription mentioning Gallio has been found at Delphi on the other side of the Gulf of Corinth. It offers one of the few possibilities of dating Paul's work. It indicates that Gallio came to Corinth as proconsul in either A.D. 51 or 52; and since Acts seems to imply that he had only recently acquired that position when Paul was brought before him, Paul must have come to Corinth about A.D. 50.

A re-used paving block found near the city's two theaters preserves an inscription which says that the pavement was the work of Erastus, who was commissioner of public works (*aedilis*). He is generally identified with the Erastus who became a disciple and co-worker of Paul (Acts 19. 22). In Rom. 16. 23 Paul calls him the *oikonomos* or 'chamberlain' of the city. He was thus an important official and an exception to the apostle's statement that not many wise or mighty or noble men after the flesh are called (1 Cor. 1. 26).

Rome

Paul landed in Italy at Puteoli (Acts 28. 13) on the north shore of the Bay of Naples, and found there Christian brethren with whom he stayed for a week before going on to the capital. This was not far from Pompeii, the city which within twenty years was to be covered with volcanic stone and dust from a sudden eruption of Mt. Vesuvius (in A.D. 79). In the ruins of this town we are accorded the most complete view of the life of an ancient town which archaeology has provided. The typical public buildings of the time are all there, but most interesting are the numerous private houses and shops which provide insight into the common life of the population. Among the shops, for example, are those of the silversmiths, grocers, bakers, dyers, a blacksmith, a surgeon, a sculptor, a tanner, and even a purveyor of hot drinks. Architecture was generally of brick covered with stucco; and the walls of public buildings and private houses were painted, often with elaborate compositions from history and mythology. The presence of Jews in the town is indicated by a wall-painting which probably depicts the judgment of Solomon (1 Kings 3. 16–28). There is also a Jewish inscription scratched on a wall, which reads 'Sodoma, Gomora'.

Until recently there was no evidence that there had been Christians in the city. A Christian interpretation has been suggested for a cryptic inscription discovered at Pompeii in 1936 and known from other sources also. But the interpretation is not certain, and little historical weight can be laid upon it. Just before the Second World War the impression of what appeared to be a cross was found in a house, and this is stronger evidence for Christians in Pompeii. Yet if there were Christians, we may safely say that they were few in number; otherwise more traces of them would have been discovered.

Rome itself in Paul's day is generally reckoned as having had a population of over a million. An inscription found in the city's port, Ostia, in 1941 says that in A.D. 14 the population was 4,100,000, but this must surely include all the inhabitants of the surrounding area.

Most of the people in ancient Rome lived in large apartment houses, the height of which, on main streets, was limited by a decree of Caesar Augustus to 70 feet. So many people had crowded into the city that the problem of supporting them was most difficult, and unemployment was severe. Much of the work was done by slaves, captured in the empire's wars. Elaborate measures were taken to keep the poor who were not slaves fed and contented by a system of food rationing, gifts of grain, and elaborate entertainments. The Circus Maximus and other similar structures were built for chariot races. After its enlargement by Nero (A.D. 54–68) the Circus Maximus seated some 250,000 spectators.

The Roman Forum, the center of the world in Paul's day, lay between the two central hills of the seven on which Rome was built. One entered it on the eastern end at the point where the Arch of Titus now stands. This was erected in A.D. 81 in honor of the conqueror of Jerusalem, and on its interior shows the booty, taken from the Temple in A.D. 70, being carried in a triumphal procession into Rome.

Near the eastern end of the Forum is the Colosseum, the greatest building of ancient and modern Rome. It was not standing in Paul's day, but was completed by Titus in A.D. 80. It was originally known as the Flavian amphitheater. It was erected on the site of an artificial lake in the middle of the gardens of Nero's palace, where Christians were tortured and burned in A.D. 64. The Colosseum once accommodated 50,000 spectators, who viewed a variety of bloody combats which took the lives of many gladiators and Christian martyrs, not to speak of thousands of wild animals.

The earliest evidence for Christians in Rome comes from cemeteries. By Roman law all places of burial had to be outside the city limits. Consequently many cemeteries have been found along the highways leading into the city. During the 1st century A.D. the Romans customarily cremated their dead and placed their ashes in urns, which were deposited in specially prepared vaults or mausoleums. In the 2nd century burial became a regular custom, and wealthy people began to use elaborately decorated sarchophagi. Jews and Christians did not favor cremation, probably because of their views concerning the resurrection of the dead. Instead they buried in underground chambers which for convenience were turned into galleries or catacombs. Several Jewish catacombs have been found in the environs of Rome. The fact that they were Jewish is most frequently revealed by the symbols on the walls, the most common of which is the menorah or seven-branched candlestick.

The Christian catacombs were far more numerous and elaborate. At least 35 have been discovered around the outskirts of the city, and the total length of their galleries has been calculated at more than 500 miles. The oldest burials in them were not made much before A.D. 150, some eighty to ninety years after Paul's death. Earlier catacombs may exist, but if so they are probably within the present city in areas which were not inhabited before the great suburban extensions of the 2nd and 3rd centuries. The walls of the underground galleries are lined with tombs, one above the other. Horizontal recesses were cut into the soft volcanic tufa, and the bodies, wrapped in Jewish fashion with lengths of cloth, were laid in the recesses, and the openings were closed with bricks or marble slabs. A more elaborate tomb was often made by cutting a semi-circular recess into the wall and then chiseling out a place for the body, which was covered with a horizontal slab.

While the catacombs are well known as places where Christians worshipped secretly during times of persecution, they are also important for the study of early Christian art. Indeed, for the 2nd and 3rd centuries A.D. they are the main sources for this study. Many of the designs and motifs were simply borrowed from pagan art, including little winged figures known as Erotes or Amoretti, which by Renaissance times were interpreted as cherubs. One of the most common Christian symbols was, of course, the fish. This had been used in pagan art, but the Christians made use of it because the five letters of the Greek word for 'fish' were the first letters in the five Greek words which meant 'Jesus Christ, Son of God, Savior'. Another common figure in early Christian art was that of the Good Shepherd, in which Christ was shown as a youth carrying a lamb over his shoulders. This figure appears over the baptistry in the early church at Dura on the Euphrates, and its finest example in Rome is a small statue of about the same period (3rd century A.D.).

The traditional tomb of the apostle Paul is under the altar of the Church of 'St. Paul Outside the Walls'. The first structure erected there was by Constantine, but this was subsequently enlarged into a monumental building which was dedicated by Pope Siricius at the very end of the 4th century. The site was in an ancient Roman cemetery, to judge from the tombs unearthed there in 1838.

Perhaps the most interesting search for early Christian remains in Rome has been that under the crypts and altar of the Church of St. Peter. According to tradition, both Peter and Paul were martyred in Rome toward the end of Nero's reign, between about A.D. 64 and 68. The traditional tomb of Peter was beneath the altar of St. Peter's, the central church of Roman Catholicism. In 1941 explorations and excavations were begun under the church when a fitting place was being sought for the tomb of Pope Pius XI. One of the first achievements of the investigation has been the new study of the first church erected on the site by Constantine in the early 4th century.

Then in the debris beneath the floor-level of the Constantinian edifice, and under the present nave of St. Peter's, two rows of mausoleums were found in which wealthy Roman families buried their dead between the 2nd and 4th centuries. Very few Christians were buried here, and those who were date for the most part from the 4th century. One small mausoleum, however, was acquired in the 3rd century by Christians, who covered the vault and walls with a single mosaic plan. These are the earliest Christian tomb-mosaics yet found. Overhead in the vault is a figure of Helios (the sun), drawn on a chariot pulled by four fiery horses and holding in his left hand an orb, depicting the world. This pagan figure was probably used to represent Christ as 'The Sun of Righteousness, the Sun of Salvation'.

Another pagan mausoleum was taken over by a Christian family at the end of the 3rd century. In it, by a pagan painting of the god Apollo, the Christians have portrayed two heads, one above the other. The lower is traced in red lead and partly re-done in charcoal. It shows an old man with bald head, pointed beard, and deeply furrowed brow. The letters PETRUS by the head identify him as Peter, and the name is followed by a prayer to the apostle, requesting his intercession for all Christians buried near his body. The upper head was probably meant to represent either Paul or Christ, but the identification is uncertain.

Under the present altar and the *Confessio Petri* are the remains of the memorial built by Constantine over the traditional tomb of St. Peter. Below that is a still earlier memorial, erected about A.D. 160 in an open area surrounded by pagan mausoleums. This was the 'trophy' or memorial mentioned by the priest Gaius, who wrote at the end of the 2nd century against the heresy of one Proclus in Asia Minor. The latter was a Montanist who believed that the world was soon coming to an end, and to support the legitimacy of his claim that his beliefs were founded on ancient church tradition he pointed to the tombs of Philip and his four daughters in Hierapolis in Asia. Gaius countered by saying: 'But I can show you the trophies of the Apostles. For whether you go to the Vatican, or along the Ostian way, you will find the trophies of those who founded the Church of Rome.' [1] In other words, Gaius is able to show in Rome the memorials to Peter and Paul.

Below the site of the monument built about A.D. 160 there were still earlier burials, some perhaps as early as A.D. 70, and also a square cavity or hollow. In the latter were some bones which had once belonged to an elderly man of powerful physique, but no actual grave seems to have been found. Thus, as Pope Pius XII stated, it is

[1] Eusebius, *Church History*, II. 25. 7.

impossible to identify these bones as those of Peter with any degree of certainty.

The precise significance of these discoveries for the location of Peter's tomb is somewhat debated. While it is now generally agreed that Peter probably did come to Rome later in his life and there suffered martyrdom, some Protestant scholars are not sure that his tomb is under the Church of St. Peter. The persecution of Nero was such that there is always the possibility that Peter's body was not identified or recovered. On the other hand, the place where the apostle was martyred was doubtless remembered. Hence it is possible to interpret the 2nd century memorial deep under the present altar of St. Peter's as simply a cenotaph which commemorated the place where the martyrdom took place. There is no evidence of a special interest in Christian relics or burial places before the end of the 2nd century, and thus it is possible that Peter's grave is and will remain unknown.

The Church in the World

The Roman world which Christianity entered was as filled with various religious beliefs as our own. Most of the people were believers in polytheism, that is, in many gods who were conceived as personal beings but were actually the powers and principles of nature. Educated people were much more sophisticated in their beliefs. The Epicureans, for example, denied that the gods intervene directly in the world. They do not need our worship, but it is natural to us to give it. The highest human good is pleasure, attained by a life of simplicity and temperance. The Stoics taught that God was the reason of the universe, and that every person has a spark of this divine mind or world-soul within him. By this he ought to live, and not be a slave of his passions. Since all men possess this divine spark, they ought to live together as citizens who share a common idealism. To Virgil the new era inaugurated by Augustus seemed to embody the ideal of a truly universal community based upon the indestructible elements of human personality beyond distinctions of race and color.

Such lofty ideas, however, had little effect upon the common man's religion. Polytheism, with its numerous gods, was always tolerant of new divinities, and the triumph of Hellenic culture meant a thorough-going syncretism. Numerous cults of Greek, Asian, and Egyptian origin were imported into Rome. These were the 'mystery' religions, into which the devotees were inducted by special rites of initiation. Their origin lay in the old nature-religion, with its worship of the dying–rising vegetation god, now adapted to secure renewal of some sort for the individual soul. In this religious atmosphere the cult of emperor-worship was also fostered, and promoted as a means of unifying the empire. In the eastern provinces it had been the custom since the days of Alexander the Great to deify the rulers during and after their life-time. The worship of Augustus and the succeeding Caesars was therefore nothing particularly new, though an innovation in Rome itself.

Judaism in this world was looked down upon as a horrible religion, since what to the Roman polytheist was highest and holiest was condemned by the Jew as accursed. Nevertheless, the Jews were considered a nation by the Romans, and as such were accorded certain privileges. In all lands there were many Gentiles who either obeyed or were influenced by the Mosaic laws, and yet Judaism never proved the threat to paganism that Christianity was to be. As Gibbon put it, Judaism was a religion 'admirably fitted for defense, but never designed for conquest'.

Christianity from the outset had a far less favored position than Judaism because it was regarded simply as a sect which had broken away from Judaism, and was not subject to the legal protection accorded a nation or people. While the Jews were released from the obligation to worship the gods and the emperor, this freedom was not extended to the Christians, and they were eventually persecuted for what was regarded as high treason.

Unlike Judaism, however, Christianity considered the spread of the Gospel as a sacred duty, and it had the strength to break through the barriers which stood in its way. While educated people despised the new religion as a superstition, and the masses hated it as 'atheism' and attributed every reversal in national fortunes to the wrath of the gods at its spread, the movement could not be stopped. In the breakdown of paganism the Gospel offered a new hope and a new security, especially for the poor and depressed. In the long run also it was able to wage a successful battle for the mind of the pagan intellectual. The dreams of the new order of Augustus Caesar, based upon the classical idealism, virtually collapsed in the 3rd century, and the Christian doctrines of man and society gradually became a doctrine of salvation in a dying culture.

Maps, Texts, and Illustrations

Maps

WHA, Plates XIIC, D, XV, XVI; Grollenberg, Endpaper II

Texts

(p. 169) *Monumentum Ancyranum*: C. K. Barrett, *The New Testament Background: Selected Documents* (London, 1957), pp. 1–5

Illustrations (The references are to Figures)

(p. 165) The Church of the Holy Sepulcher: *WHA*, 71; (5th ed.), 79

(p. 165) Dura-Europos: *ECW*, 51–2, 71–2; Grollenberg, 4; Wright, 192; *WHA*, 70; (5th ed.), 78

(p. 166) Antioch in Syria: Grollenberg, 391; Wright, 194

(p. 168) The Chalice of Antioch: Wright, 195

(p. 169) *Monumentum Ancyranum*: Wright, 197

(p. 170) Ephesus: Grollenberg, 400; Wright, 200–1; *WHA*, 67; (5th ed.), 75

(p. 172) The Via Egnatia: Grollenberg, 395

(p. 174) Thessalonica Inscription: Wiseman, 99

(p. 174) Athens: Grollenberg, 404; *WHA*, 66; (5th ed.), 74

(p. 175) Corinth: Grollenberg, 402

(p. 177) The Erastus Inscription: Wright, 209

(p. 178) Pompeii: *WHA*, 68; (5th ed.), 76

(p. 179) The Arch of Titus: Grollenberg, 406–8; Wright, 214

(p. 180) The Catacombs: *ECW*, 54–60, 62–7, 82–93; Wright, 216

(p. 182) Excavations under St. Peter's: *ECW*, 74–5

INDEX OF BIBLICAL REFERENCES

Genesis:
1 . . . 4
1. 26 . . 5
2 . . . 25
2. 9 . . 14
3. 22 . . 5
3. 24 . . 83
6–9 . . 25
10. 8 ff. . . 26
11 . . 26
11. 10 ff. . 22
11. 31 . . 22
12 . . 28
13. 10 . . 30
13. 18 . . 28
14 . . 31 f.
14. 13 . . 24
15. 2 ff. . . 25
17. 1 . . 32
19. 24–28 . 30
21. 34 . . 21
23 . . 31
23. 2 . . 29
23. 17 . . 28
24. 10 . . 21 f.
25. 20 . . 22
25. 30–34 . 25
26 . . 21
26. 23 . . 28
27. 33 . . 25
28. 5 . . 22
28. 10 . 22, 28
28. 10–17 . 5
28. 17 . . 80
28. 18 ff. . 31
30. 31–31. 12 . 25
30. 35 . . 25
31. 20, 24 . 22
31. 44 ff. . 31
33. 18 . . 28
33. 20 . . 31
34 . . 46
35. 1 . . 28
35. 27 . . 29
37. 17 . . 28
39. 5 . . 34

Genesis:
39. 7 ff. . . 35
40. 2 . . 34
40. 20 ff. . 35
41. 8 . . 35
41. 40 . . 71
41. 42 f. . . 35
43. 32 . . 35
46. 28 ff. . 36
46. 34 . . 35
47. 11 . . 36
47. 13 ff. . 37
49. 25 . . 8
50. 2 f. . . 35
50. 22 . . 35
50. 26 . . 35

Exodus:
1. 11 . 29, 38, 44
2. 16 ff. . . 40
3 . . . 32
6. 3 . . 32
7–12 . . 35
12. 40 . . 51
13. 17 f. . . 39
14. 2 . . 39
15. 27 . . 40
17. 1 . . 40
18. 1 ff. . . 40
19. 16 ff. . 8
20. 1 f. . . 56
20. 3 . . 57
20. 4 . . 17
21–23 . . 57
23. 20–33 . 57
34. 13 . . 57
34. 17 . . 17

Leviticus:
7. 32 . . 15
26 . . 57
26. 30 . . 14

Numbers:
1 . . . 41
10. 29 . . 40

Numbers:
10. 35 f. . . 41
11. 24–29 . 62
13. 22 . 29, 37
2. 17. . . 31
21. 22 . . 31
22–24 . . 42
24. 1 . . 43
26 . . . 41
26. 29–33 . 101
33 . . . 40
33. 9, 12, 14 . 40

Deuteronomy:
1. 2 . . 40
4. 19 . . 6
6. 4 f. . . 142
7. 5 . . 7
7. 22 . . 44
8. 9 . . 79
12. 3 . . 7
16. 21 . . 7
18. 10 . . 12
23, 17 f. . . 13
26. 5 . . 22
27–28 . . 57
31. 9–13 . . 57
33. 13 ff. . 8

Joshua:
6–9 . . 43
8. 28 . . 48
8. 30–35 . . 46
8. 34 . . 57
10 . . 43, 49 f.
10–12 . . 45
11 . . . 43
11. 10 . . 50
11. 10–13 . 49
11. 13 . . 44
11. 22 . . 44
12. 16 . . 48
13 . . . 44
15. 21–62 . 77
17. 16 . . 59
18. 1 . . 58

Joshua:
24 . . . 46
24. 2 . . 56
24. 2–13 . . 57
24. 14, 26 . 57

Judges:
1 . . . 43 f.
1. 19 . 44, 59
1. 22–26 . . 48
1. 27 ff. . . 44
2. 13 . . 9
2. 20–23 . . 44
4. 11 . . 40
5 . . . 61
5. 19 . . 61
10. 6 . . 9
11. 26 . . 51
20 . . . 67

1 Samuel:
1 ff. . . 58
2. 12 ff. . . 15
2. 27–36 . . 64
4 . . . 58
7. 4 . . 9
8. 4 . . 97
9. 12 . . 13
10. 5 . 62, 66
12. 10 . . 9
13–14 . . 68
13. 3 . . 66
13. 19–22 . 58
14. 21 . . 66
14. 37 . . 64
28. 6, 15 . . 64
31 . . . 68
31. 10 . 9, 61 f.

2 Samuel:
5. 9 . 72, 77
7 . . . 64
7. 14 . . 85
8 . . . 69
8. 16–18 . . 70
12 . . . 64
15. 18 . . 69
20. 23–26 . 70
22. 11 . . 83
23. 13, 24 . 72
24 . . . 42

1 Kings:
1 . . . 73
3. 4 . . 13
3. 16–28 . . 178
4. 6 . . 71
4. 7 ff., 22 f. . 76
5. 13 ff. . . 78
6. 1 . . 50
6. 4, 35 . . 81
7. 13 ff. . . 84
7. 21 . . 80
7. 23 ff., 46 . 84
8. 6 . . 82
8. 27–30 . . 87
9. 15–19, 21 f. . 78
9. 26 . 76, 79
10. 22 . . 76
10. 26 . . 97
10. 28 f. . . 76
11. 5 . . 9
11. 14–22 . 90
11. 29 ff. . 64
12. 25 . . 91
12. 26 ff. . 92
14. 1 ff. . . 64
14. 25 f. . . 93
16. 8 ff., 21–28 94
16. 33 . . 7
18. 3 . . 71
18. 19 . . 7, 9
19. 1–8 . . 40
19. 11 f. . . 8
20. 23 . . 44
22. 39 . . 96
22. 47 . . 90

2 Kings:
1. 1 . . 97
1. 2 . . 7
3. 4 ff. . . 97
3. 27 . . 12
8. 7–15 . . 98
12. 17–13.23 . 98
14. 22 . . 102
14. 25, 28 . 100
15. 19 . . 103
15. 29 . 104 f.
15. 30 . . 105
16. 6 . . 102
16. 7, 9 . . 104
16. 17 . . 84
17. 3 f. . . 105
17. 24 . . 108
18–20 . . 108
18. 14 . . 110
18. 18 . . 71
18. 26 . . 120
18. 34 . . 103
19. 13 . . 103
20. 20 . . 112
21. 3, 7 . . 7
22–23 . . 118
23. 13 . . 9
23. 29 . . 119
24. 1 . . 119
25. 1–7 . . 122
25. 1 . . 125
25. 13 . . 84

1 Chronicles:
7. 14–19 . . 101
10. 10 . . 62

2 Chronicles:
3. 5 . . 81
4. 6 . . 84
11. 5–10 . . 110
12. 2 ff. . . 93
14. 5 . . 14
14. 9 ff. . . 94
20. 1 . . 90
28. 18 . . 105
29–31 . . 108
32. 30 . . 112
33. 11 . . 116
34. 3–7 . . 117
34. 3 . . 117
34. 4, 7 . . 14

Ezra:
1. 2–4 . 103 f.
4. 8–6, 18 . 136
6. 3–5 . . 130
7. 7, 12–26 . 136
10. 6–8 . . 135

Nehemiah:
3. 1 . . 135
7. 66 ff. . . 129
9. 6 . . 6
12. 22 . . 135
12. 22 f. . . 133

Job:
3. 8 . . . 3
41 . . . 3

Psalms:
2 . . . 86
2. 7 . . 85
18. 10 . . 83
18. 13 f. . . 8
29 . . . 8
29. 9 . . 8
48. 2 . . 7
50. 12 f. . . 86
68. 4 . . 8

Psalms:
74. 13 f. . . 3
78. 12 . . 36
89. 10 . . 3
110 . . 86
148 . . 6

Proverbs:
22. 17–24. 22 . 140

Isaiah:
6 . . . 5
7. 3 . . 75
8. 6 . . 75
15–16 . . 117
17. 8 . . 14
22. 9 . . 112
22. 11 . 74, 112
22. 15 ff. . . 114
22. 21 . . 72
27. 1 . . 3
27. 9 . . 14
51. 9 . . 3

Jeremiah:
1. 2 . . 117
7. 12 ff. . . 58
26. 2 . . 62
26. 6 ff. . . 58
26. 15 . . 62
28–29 . . 123
28. 15 . . 62
32. 9 . . 116
34. 7 . . 124
38. 4 . . 125
47. 5, 7 . . 120
52. 28 f. . . 122

Ezekiel:
6. 4, 6 . . 14
10–11 . . 88
10. 20 . . 83
28. 14 . . 7
40. 5–16 . . 78
41. 8 . . 80
41. 18 ff. . 81
43. 13–17 . 83

Hosea:
2. 16 f. . . 101
2. 17 . . 8
6. 1–3 . . 11

Amos:
3. 15 . . 96
6. 4 . . 96
9. 3 . . 3

Micah:
4. 8 . . 73
5. 14 . . 7

Nahum:
3. 8 . . 115

Habakkuk:
1. 12 . . 12
2. 19 . . 15

Matthew:
1. 11 f. . . 123
2. 1 . . 158
12. 24 . . 7
18. 15–17 . 156

Mark:
7. 24, 31 . . 159
8. 27 . . 158
13. 2 . . 153
15 . . . 151

Luke:
1. 5 . . 158
2. 1–3 . . 157
3. 1 . . 158

John:
3. 21 . . 156
14. 17 . . 156
15. 26 . . 156
16. 13 . . 156
19. 5, 13 . . 152

Acts:
4. 32–37 . . 155
4. 32 . . 156
6. 2, 5 . . 156
9. 2 . . 156
11. 26 . . 167
13. 14–14. 24 . 168
15. 12, 30 . 156
16. 13, 19 ff. . 173
17. 6, 17 . . 174
17. 19–31 . 175
18. 2 f. . . 176
18. 12–17 . 177
19. 13, 18 . 172
19. 22 . . 177
19. 27 . . 170
19. 31 . . 172
19. 35 . 171 f.
21. 27 ff. . . 151
25. 23 ff. . 148 f.
28. 13 . . 178

Romans:
16. 23 . . 177

1 Corinthians:
1. 26 . . 178
10. 25 . . 177
16. 8 f. . . 171

Ephesians:
2. 2 . . 156
3. 10 . . 156

1 John:
4. 6 . . 156

Revelation:
21. 1 . . 3

GENERAL INDEX

Abraham (Abram), 21–25, 28–32
Adon, 8
Adonis, 11
Adoption, 25
After-life, 15 f., 153 f., 180
Agriculture, 10, 53, 59, 67
Ahab, 94–97, 99
Ahaz, 75, 84, 102, 104 f.
Ai, 43, 48, 50
Akhnaton (Amenophis IV), 45
Akkadian language, 83, 120 f.
Albright, W. F., 48, 94 n., 124
Alexander the Great, 136 f., 139, 171, 174, 185
Alexandria, 138, 166
Alphabet, 41, 54
Alt, A., 32 n., 55 n.
Altars, sacrificial, 13, 19, 29, 83, 89, 115, 171
Altars of incense, 14, 19
Amen-em-opet, Wisdom of, 140, 145 f.
Amenophis IV, *see* Akhnaton
Amman, 90, 158 n.
Ammon, 42, 51, 54 f., 69, 90, 96, 116
Amon, 62, 93
Amorites, 23 f., 28, 32
Amphictyones, 56
Amraphel, 31
Anath, 9 f., 19, 134 f.
Ancestor-worship, 14
Ancyra (Ankara), 169
Antioch in Syria, 166–168, 187
Antioch of Pisidia, 168–170
Antiochus IV (Epiphanes), 136
Antonia, Tower of, 151 f., 163
Aphek (Ras el-'Ain), 120
Aphrodite, 11
apilu, 63 f.
'*Apiru*, see *Hapiru*
Apollo, 167, 176, 183
Apsu, 1 f.
Arabah, 41, 78 f., 89
Arabic language, 141
Arabs, 41, 116, 127
Aram-Naharaim, 22
Aramaeans, 22 f., 54, 69, 90
Aramaic language, 120, 130 f., 136, 138, 141
Ararat, 27
Architecture, 53, 67 f., 91
  classical Greek, 78, 174 f.
  Hellenistic, 138, 167, 170, 171 f.
  Phoenician, 72, 77 f., 79 ff., 96
  Roman, 170, 173, 176 f., 178, 179 f.
Areopagus, 175
Ark, Noah's, 26 f.
Ark of the Covenant, 41, 55, 58, 72, 82
Arsames (Arsham), 133 f.
Arslan Tash, 96
Art, 9
  Canaanite, 13, 61
  Damascene, 96
  early Christian, 166, 181 f.
  Egyptian, 13, 81
  Phoenician, 80 ff., 89, 96
Artaxerxes I, 131, 136
Artaxerxes II, 136
Artemis, 170 ff.
Ashdod, 54, 109, 120
Asherah, 6 f., 9, 14
Ashkelon, 29, 54, 120, 122 f.
Ashtoreth, 9 f.
Asiarchs, 172
Asshurbanapal, 26, 115 ff., 127
Asshuretelilani, 117
Asshur-rabi II, 70
Assyria, 26, 53, 70, 96, 98, 100, 102–106, 108–110, 115–119
Astarte, 9, 94
Astrology, 19, 64
Athena, 175
Athens, 149, 174 f., 187
Augustus Caesar, 148, 157, 169, 173, 176, 179, 185 f.
Avaris, 36 f.
Avigad, N., 114
Azariah, *see* Uzziah
Azekah, 124
Azriau of Yauda, 103, 106

Baal, 2, 7 ff., 14 f., 20, 92, 101
Baal-zebul, 7
Baal-zephon, 39
Babel, Tower of, 26
Babylonian Chronicle, 118 f., 121 f., 127
  creation story, 1 ff., 19
  Empire, New, 111, 116, 118 ff., 122 ff., 129 f., 132
  Empire, Old, 23, 26
  flood story, 26 ff., 33
  New Year Festival, 85, 88

Babylonian Chronicle (*contd.*)
religion, 1 f., 11, 42 f., 64, 84
Bagoas, 133
Balaam, 42 f.
Balak, 42 f.
Baptism, 155, 165
baru, 42 f.
Bashan, 90
Beast, in Revelation, 3
Bedouin, 36, 56, 142
Beersheba, 28 f.
Beni-Hasan relief, 28, 33
Benjaminites, at Mari, 23, 63
Berlin texts, 29, 33
Bethel, 28 f., 48 ff., 55, 67, 92, 128 f.
Bethlehem, 157, 165
Beth-shan, 15, 19, 43 f., 55, 61, 65, 69
Beth-shemesh, 76, 123, 126
Beth-zur, 129, 137
Black Obelisk of Shalmaneser, 98, 106 f.
Boaz, 80 f.
Boghazköy, 31
Bronze Age, 50, 53, 94, 112
Brownlee, W. H., 155 n.
Brussels texts, 29, 33
Bulls, 82, 92, 106, 170
Burial of the Dead, 12, 16, 26, 28, 31, 35, 111 f., 113–115, 180–184
Byblos, 62

Caesar, Julius, 173
Caesarea, 148 f., 163
Cambyses, 133
Camels, 21, 60
Canaan, Canaanites,
city-states, 44 f., 55, 60 ff., 69
conquest of, 43 ff., 55
culture, 29 f., 61, 91
Egyptian province, 45, 53
invasions of, 53 f.
patriarchs in, 28 ff.
religion, 2, 6 ff., 25, 32, 84, 92
state slaves, 78
Capernaum (Khan Minyeh or Tell Hum), 159, 163
Carchemish, 22, 119, 122
'Casemate' wall, 99
Catacombs, 180 ff., 187
Census, 41 f., 157 f.
Chalice of Antioch, 168, 187
Chaos, 1 f., 84 f.
Chariots and horses, 44, 50, 61, 75 f., 96 f., 105, 108
Chebar (Kabar), R., 132
Chemosh, 97
Cherethites, 69
Cherubim, 81–83, 181
Chester Beatty Papyri, 161, 163
Christianity, beliefs, 180, 186
Chronology, New Testament, 158, 177
Old Testament, 50 f., 94 n., 122
Church buildings, 165 f., 167, 170, 176
Cilicia, 75 f.
Clermont-Ganneau, C., 113
Codex, 161
Sinaiticus, 142, 163
Vaticanus, 142
Coinage, 131 f., 145
Colonies, Roman, 169, 173, 176
Conscription, 78
Constantine, 165 f., 181 ff.
Copper, 31, 39, 41, 53, 59, 79, 102
Corinth, 175–178, 187
Covenant, 32, 46 f., 55 ff., 66
Book of, 57
Creation stories, 1 ff., 19, 25
Cremation, 180
Cross, F. M., 77 n.
Cyprus, 54
Cyrus, 129–131
Cylinder, 129, 145
decree of, 130 f.
Dagan, 63
Damascus, 69 f., 90, 96 f., 98 ff., 104, 106
Dan, 92
Daniel, book of, 140, 144
David, 55, 60, 62, 66, 69 ff., 77, 79, 90, 97
Tower of, 151, 163
Davidic dynasty, 90, 108, 117, 131
Dead Sea, 30 f., 154
Dead Sea Scrolls, 142–146, 154–157, 162
Debir (Tell Be't Mirsim), 45, 93, 121, 123, 126
Deborah, Song of, 61
Decapolis, 158
Demetrius, 170 f.
Deportation, 104, 130
Deuteronomy, 57, 118, 143, 155
Dibon, 97
dikrona, 130
Dispersion of the Jews, 138, 164, 167 f., 173, 177 f., 180
District organization, 76 f.
Divination, 12, 19, 42 f., 64
Dophkah (Serabit el-Khadem), 40
Dor, 44, 54
Dothan, 28 f.
Driver, G. R., 133 n.
Dura-Europos, 165 f., 181, 187
Dying-rising god, myth ff., 185

Ea, 26
Ebenezer, 58
Ecbatana, 131
Ecce Homo Arch, 152, 163
Ecclesiastes, 140, 143 f.
Ecstasy, 62
Eden, Garden of, 14, 26
Edom, 40, 42, 53, 55, 69, 90, 93, 102, 105, 116
Egnatia, Via, 172 ff., 187

Egypt,
 and Assyria, 96, 108, 115, 119
 and Babylon, 119, 122, 125
 and Syria-Palestine, 28, 30, 36, 45, 53, 61, 93 f., 119, 136
 early evidence for Christianity, 165
 Exodus from, 38 ff.
 influence on David and Solomon, 70–72
 Jewish settlement in, 132–135
 religion, 2 f., 11, 13, 25, 62
 sojourn in, 24, 34 ff.
ekklesia, 169
Ekron, 7, 54, 108 f., 120
El, 6 ff., 11, 14, 32, 92
El Elyon, 32
Elath, *see* Ezion-geber
Elephantine papyri, 132–135, 145
Eliakim, 123, 127
Elim (Wadi Gharandel), 40
Elyon, 8, 32
Emperor-worship, 172, 185 f.
Enlil, 27
En-Rogel, 73
'Ephesian writings', 172
Ephesus, 170–172, 187
Epicureans, 184
Erastus, 177, 187
Esarhaddon, 115
Esau, 25
Esdraelon, Plain of, 30, 44, 61, 77, 93, 95
Essenes, 142 f., 153–157
Esther, book of, 140 f., 143
Euphrates, R., 22, 27, 42, 62, 70, 165
Exile, The, 26, 123 f., 132
Exodus, The, 4, 30, 34, 38 ff., 46
 date of, 38, 42, 44 f., 50 f.
 tribes which took no part in, 46 f.
Ezekiel, 80 n., 88, 123, 132
Ezion-geber (Elath), 76, 79, 89, 93, 102, 105
Ezra, 135, 139
 book of, 136

Family deity, 32
Fate, 3
Fertile Crescent, 23, 70
Fertility cults, 12 f., 85, 170
 goddess, 9–11, 13, 19, 85
Fish, symbol of the, 181
Flood, The, 25–27
Fortifications,
 Ai, 48
 Beth-zur, 137
 Debir, 121
 Gezer, 30, 138
 Gibeah, 68
 Jerusalem, 72, 74 f., 149–151
 Jericho, 47
 Lachish, 111, 121
 Megiddo, 77 f., 104
 Samaria, 95 f., 99, 137, 147 f.
 Sharuhen, 93
 Shechem, 91 f.
 'the way of the land of the Philistines', 39

Gadd, C. J., 118
Galatia, 168–170
Galilee, 43, 49, 95, 104, 117, 158 f.
 Sea of, 90, 158 f.
Gallio, 177
Games, athletic, 148
Garstang, J., 47
Gath, 54, 69, 120
Gaza, 54, 93, 104, 109, 120
Gehenna, 73
Gerasa, 158 n., 163
Gezer, 30, 44 f., 49, 55, 67, 138
 Calendar, 67, 88
Gibeah, 60, 67–69, 80
Gihon, 73 f., 112 f.
Gilgamesh, 26
Ginsberg, H. L., 120
Glueck, N., 42, 78, 102
God-fearers, 167 f., 185
Gomorrah, 30
Good Shepherd theme, 166, 181
Gordon, C. H., 31 n.
Goshen, 36 f.
Grail, The Holy, 168
Greece, Greeks, 11, 54, 78
Greek language, 164, 169

Hadad, 7, 106
Hamath, 96
hammanim, 14
Hammurabi, 23, 31
Hapiru, 23 f., 38, 45
Haran, 22 f., 27 f., 119
harel, 83
Hattina (Tell Tainat), 80
Hazael, 96, 98 f.
Hazor (Tell el-Qedah), 18 n., 43, 49 f., 52, 78, 89, 104 f., 107
Heavenly host, worship of, 5 f., 115
Hebrew language, 17, 113 f., 124, 130 f., 141
Hebrews, 24, 37 f., 45
Hebron, 29, 37, 45
Hellenism, 136 ff., 147, 167, 169, 185
Herod Agrippa, 150
Herod Antipas, 158
Herod the Great, 147 ff., 158
Herodotus, 117 f.
Hezekiah, 75, 108–110, 112, 115 f.
 tunnel of, 112, 127
Hierapolis, 131
High places, 13 f., 30
High priest, 131, 135
Hinnom, 73, 150
Hiram, king of Tyre, 80
History, 4, 18
Hittites, 26, 31, 42, 53, 59
Hobab, 40
Holiness Code, 57
Holy Sepulcher, Church of the, 150, 165, 187
Homer, 54
Horeb, 39 f.
Horites, 24
Hosea, 11
Hoshea, 105
Hurrians, 24
Hyksos, 29, 36–38, 46, 50 f.

Hyrcanus, John, 138, 147

Idumaea, 137, 147
Images, 7, 9, 15, 17 f., 87, 92, 170 f., 175
Iron, 53, 59 f., 79
Isaac, 21, 25, 28, 32
Isaiah, 75, 112, 114
 book of, 143 f.
Ishtar, 11
Isis, 11
Israel,
 confederation of tribes, 46, 55 ff.
 mentioned on *stele* of Merneptah, 44
 Northern Kingdom, 7, 46, 72, 76 f., 90–106, 117
 united kingdom, 66 ff., 108, 117, 119
Ivory, 61, 65, 81 f., 89, 96, 109

Jachin, 80 f.
Jacob, 21, 23, 25, 28 f., 32
Jaffa Gate, citadel at, 150 f.
Jebusites, 72, 74, 79
Jehoiachin, 123
 tablets, 120, 122 f., 127
Jehoiakim, 119, 121 f.
Jehoshaphat, 77
Jehu, 96, 98 f., 101
Jephthah, 51
Jeremiah, 116 ff., 120, 125
 book of, 143
Jericho, 43, 47 f., 50, 52, 112
Jeroboam I, 90–92
Jeroboam II, 100, 103
Jerusalem,
 Canaanite city, 29, 32, 43, 45, 49, 55, 72, 74, 79, 88
 capital of province of Judah, 131, 133–136
 capital of Southern Kingdom, 90, 93, 95, 109 f., 112–115
 capital of united Israel, 69, 72–75, 77, 79 ff., 88, 92
Jerusalem (*contd.*)
 fall of, 84, 122, 126, 129, 138
 under Herod the Great, 147 f., 149–153
Jethro, 40
Jewish Revolts,
 First, 150, 159
 Second, 143, 159
Jezebel, 7, 9, 94
Jezreel, 60 f.
Job, book of, 140
Johanan, 133, 135
John the Baptist, 155
John, Gospel of, 144, 160
Johns, C. N., 151
Jordan Valley, 30
Joseph, 34–37
Josephus, 73, 82, 84, 147 f., 150 f., 153 f.
Joshua, 43 ff.
Josiah, 117 ff., 134
Jotham, 102
Judaea, 158 f.
Judah, province of, 128 ff., 133
 Southern Kingdom, 43, 46, 49, 72, 77, 90 f., 93, 98, 102 ff., 108 ff.
Judaism, 180, 185
Judith, book of, 141

Kadesh, battle of, 42
Kadesh-barnea, 40
Karnak, 39, 93
Kenites, 40 f.
Kenyon, Miss K. M., 47
Khirbet Qumran, 154
Kidron, 73, 150
Kingship, 2, 54 f., 82, 84–86
King's Highway, 31
Kiriath-arba (Hebron), 29
Kraeling, E. G., 134 n.

Laban, 25
Lab'ayu, 46
Lachish (Tell ed-Duweir), 15, 20, 45, 49 f., 52, 77, 110–112, 121, 124–126, 126 f., 137
 letters, 124–126, 127
Lachish (*contd.*)
 relief of Sennacherib, 110, 126 f.
Lamentations, 126
Latin language, 169
Law, 9, 12, 24 f., 31, 57 f., 164
Lehmann, M. R., 31 n.
Leviathan (Lotan), 2, 84
Lewy, J., 32 n.
Love songs, Egyptian, 140, 145
Ludlul bel Nemeqi, 140, 145

Maccabees, 137 f., 147, 149
Machpelah, 16, 28, 31
Magic, 19, 35, 43, 85 f., 172
Makkedah, 49
Mamre, 28 f., 31
Man, understanding of, 2, 5
Manasseh, King, 7, 115–117, 126
Manasseh, clans of, 101
Manuscripts, New Testament, 160 ff.
 Old Testament, 141 ff.
Marduk, king of the gods, 2, 129 f., 131
Mari, 22 f., 32 f., 62–65
Marisa (Mareshah, Tell Sandahannah), 137, 146
Medes, 118
Mediterranean, 54 f., 115
Megiddo, 13, 19, 30, 33, 44, 55, 61, 65, 77 f., 88, 93, 98 f., 104, 110, 117, 119, 128 f.
Men, the god, 170
Menahem, 103
Mendenhall, G. E., 56
Merneptah, 44, 49
Mesha, 12, 97
Mesopotamia, Christianity and, 164
 north, home of the patriarchs, 22–28
 unidentified kings of, 31
Messiah, 123, 155 ff., 169
Midian, 40 f., 60
Miletus, 148

Millo, 77
Mishnah, 153
Mizpah, 128
Moab, 12, 42, 53, 55, 69, 90, 97, 116 f.
Moabite Stone, 97, 106 f.
Monumentum Ancyranum, 169, 186 f.
Moses, 34, 40
Mot, 10
Mother-goddess, 7, 14, 18, 20, 170
Mozah, 131
Murashu archives, 132, 145
Myth, 3 f., 9 ff., 84
Mystery religions, 185

Nabonidus, 129
Nabopolassar, 118
Nahor, 22 f.
Names, proper, 8, 22 f., 34, 101, 132
divine, 6 ff., 32, 134 f.
Nash Papyrus, 141 f.
Nativity, Church of the, 165
Nature, 1, 3 ff., 10, 18, 85
Nebuchadnezzar, 111, 119 ff., 128
Necho, 119, 122
Nehemiah, 131, 135
Nero, 176, 179, 180, 182, 184
New Year festival, 2, 85 f., 88
Nile, 36, 133
Nimrod, 26
Nineveh, 22, 24, 26, 102, 110, 115, 118
Nippur, 132, 140
Nomads, 28, 36, 41, 60
Noth, M., 55 n.
Numbers, writing of, 101 f.
Nuzi, 24 f., 32 f.

Og, 53
Old Testament, canon, 138 f.
Olives, Mount of, 73
Omri, 94 f., 98 f.
Ophel, 72 ff., 79, 149, 160
Orontes, 96 f., 167
Osiris, 11
Oxyrhynchus papyri, 161 f.

Paddan-Aram, 22 f.
Padi, 108 f.
Palestine, climate of, 10
hill country of, 28, 43 f., 46, 53, 55, 60, 66, 72, 93
Palladium, 41
Papyri, 120, 132 ff., 141 f., 157, 160 ff., 165
Parthenon, 175
Parthians, 147
Paul, St., 166 ff., 181, 183
Pausanias, 175
Pedersen, J., 56
Pekah, 105
Pelethites, 69
Pergamum, 175
Pericles, 175
Persia, 120, 129 ff., 136 f., 140
Peter, St., 182–184
Church of, 182–184, 187
Phaliga, 23
Pharisees, 153 f.
Phidias, 175
Philadelphia (Amman), 158 n., 163
Philip the Tetrarch, 158
Philippi, 172 f.
Philistines, 21, 54 f., 58 ff., 65 f., 69, 91, 105 f., 108
Phoenicia (*see also under* Art, Architecture), 6, 54, 76, 94 f., 98, 114
Phoenician language, 141
Pilate, 158
Pillars, sacred, 14, 19, 29, 31
pim, 59, 65
Pithom (Tell er-Retabeh), 38, 44
Pius XI, 182
Pius XII, 183
Plagues of Egypt, 35
Plain, cities of the, 30 f.
Pliny, 154
Poetry, Hebrew, 139
Politarchs, 174, 187
Polytheism, 1–6, 17 f., 84 ff., 115, 184 f.
Pompeii, 158 n., 178 f., 187
Population, 41 f., 91, 129, 167, 170, 179
Potiphar, 34 f.
Pottery,
alien, at Samaria, 108
burial gifts, 16, 111
evidence for dating, 42, 47, 49, 74, 77, 91, 99, 151
Israelite, 69
Philistine, 58, 65 f.
potsherds, *ostraka*, 100–102, 106 f., 124–127
stamped jars, 132
'Prime Minister', 35, 71 f.
Prophets, 62–65, 125
Prostitution, sacred, 13
Proverbs, 139 f.
Psalms, 139, 143
Ptolemies, 136
Pul, *see* Tiglath-pileser III

Qantir, 37
Qarqar, 96 f.
Qatna, 23
Quirinius, 157 f.
Qumran, 142–145, 154–157, 163

Raamses (Rameses), 29, 36, 38 f., 44, 52
Rahab, 2
Rameses II, 37 f., 42, 45
Rameses III, 61
Ras Shamra (Ugarit), 6, 9 f., 12, 15, 17, 19, 54, 139, 141
Re, 2
Recorder, 70
Red Sea, 39
Reed Sea (Yam Suph), 39
Rehoboam, 93, 110
Rephidim (Wadi Refayid), 40
Resettlement policy, 130
Reuel, 40

Roads, Roman, 159, 164, 172, 173 f., 176, 187
Robinson, E., 95
Romans, 137, 143, 147, 151, 159, 164 ff.
Rome, 164, 166, 179–184
Rowley, H. H., 31 n.
Rylands Fragment, 144, 160

Sacrifice, 12 f., 15 ff., 86 f., 133 f., 154
Sadducees, 153 f.
Samaria, 94–96, 99–102, 105 ff., 108, 117, 128 f., 137 f., 146, 147 f., 163
  ostraka, 100–102, 106 f.
Samaritans, 141
Samuel, books of, 143
Sanballat, 133
Saqqara letter, 119 ff., 127
Sargon II, 105 f., 108
Sarugi, 23
Satan, 7, 19
Saul, 44, 58, 60, 66, 67–69, 92
Scott, R. B. Y., 80 n.
Scribe, 71
Scythians, 117 f.
Sea (Yam), 2 f., 84
  bronze, 83 f., 89
Sea Peoples, 54, 65
Seals, seal impressions,
  of *baru*, 43
  of Eliakim, 123 f., 127
  of Jotham, 102, 107
  of Judah, etc., 131 f., 145
  of Pekah, 105
Seleucia, 167
Seleucids, 136
Seleucus I, 168
Sellin, E., 47
Sennacherib, 108–110, 112, 116, 126 f.
Septuagint, 138, 142, 144, 161
Seti I, inscription of, 39, 52
Shaddai, 32
Shalmaneser III, 90, 96 ff., 106
Shalmaneser V, 105
Sharon, Plain of, 30, 54
Sharuhen (Tell el-Far'ah), 93
Shebna (Shebaniah), 114 f., 127
Shechem, 28 f., 46, 50, 52, 67, 91, 94 f., 101, 138
Shema, 142
Sheol, 16
Shephelah, 110, 124
Shiloh, 55, 58, 65 ff.
Shipbuilding, 53, 76
Shishak, 93 f., 98, 106
Sidon, 54
Sihon, 53
Siloam, 112 f., 114
  inscription, 112 f., 126 f.
Silwan (Siloam), 113
Sinai, 36, 39 ff., 52
Sinuhe, 28, 33
Slavery, 78 f., 179
Smith, George, 26
Sodom, 30
Solomon, 50 f., 55, 61, 66, 71, 74 ff., 90, 97, 152
Song of Songs, 140
Sons of God,
  Canaanite deities, 5 f.
  heavenly host, 5 f.
  king, 84 f.
Stables, 78, 152
Starkey, J. L., 49, 110 f., 124
stele, 400-year, 37, 52
  of Merneptah, 44, 52
Stoics, 184 f.
Stone Age, 47
Store cities, 75, 77
Strabo, 170
Sumerians, 22, 140
Suzerainty treaties, 56 ff.
Synagogues, 159 f., 163, 177
Syncretism, 115, 117, 135, 185
Syria,
  Amorites in, 23, 28
  and Arabs, 116
  Aramaean state (Damascus), 53 f., 69 f., 90, 100
Syria (*contd.*)
  and Assyrians, 97, 102 f.
  and Babylonians, 122
  Canaanites in, 41
  and early Church, 165–168
  Egyptian control of, 53, 119
  excavations in, 6, 14 f., 80, 96
  Hittites in, 53
  and Hyksos, 36
  and Persians, 131
  and Romans, 157
  'Sea Peoples' in, 54
  Seleucid dynasty, 136 f.

Taanach, 44, 55, 61
Tabernacle, 41, 58, 72, 88
Tahpanhes (Tell Defneh), 39
Tammuz, 11
Tanis, 37 ff., 52
Tarshish, 54
Taxation, 76, 100, 131 f., 157
Teacher of Righteousness, 155, 157
Tel-abib (on R. Chebar), 132
Tell el-Amarna letters, 45 f., 52
Tell el-Far'ah (Sharuhen), 93
  (Tirzah), 94, 112
Tell en-Nasbeh (Mizpah?), 128 f.
Tell Jemmeh (Jorda?), 93
Tell Tainat (Hattina), 80, 89
Temples,
  of Artemis at Ephesus, 170 f.
  in honor of Caesar, 148 f.
  Canaanite, 15, 19 f., 30, 61 f., 81
  at Elephantine, 133 f.
  Ezekiel's, 78, 83
  Hellenistic, 137
  Herod's, at Jerusalem, 149, 152 f., 163, 179

Temples (*contd.*)
  house of deity, 15, 86 f.
  second Jerusalem, 133
  microcosm of world, 87
  Solomon's, 50, 75, 79–88, 89, 92 f.
Ten Commandments, 57, 142
Terah, 22
teraphim, 25, 33
Textual criticism, 142, 144 f.
Thebes, 115
Theodotus inscription, 160, 163
Thessalonica (Salonica), 173 f.
Thirty, The 72
Tiamat (*tehom*), 1 f., 4
Tiglath-pileser I, 53
Tiglath-pileser III, 102–105, 106
Til-Turakhi, 23
Tirzah (Tell el-Far'ah), 94
Titus, emperor, 149, 153, 179
Tjikal, 54
Tobit, book of, 141
Transjordan, 30 f., 42, 44, 51, 53, 93, 97, 104, 116, 158
Tree, sacred, 7, 14, 19, 83, 171
Trepanning, 112, 117
Tribute, 84, 103, 109 f., 116, 127
'Trophies' of the apostles, 183
Two Brothers, Tale of, 35, 51
Tyre, 7, 9, 54, 80, 94, 116
Tyropoeon, 72, 75, 149

Ugarit (Ras Shamra), 6, 23, 54
Ugaritic language, 141
'Unknown gods', 175
'Unknown Gospel', 160
Ur, 22, 27
Uruk, 26
Utnapishtim, 26 f.
Uzziah (Azariah, Azriau), 102 f., 106

Vaux, R. de, 94
Vincent, H., 151 f.
Virgil, 185

Wadi Muraba'at, 143
Wadi Tumilat, 36, 38
Wailing Wall, 152, 163
Water supply, 73 ff., 112 f.
Watzinger, C., 47
Weapons, tools, etc., 16, 53, 59 f., 68, 88, 138
Weidner, E. F., 122
Weights and measures, 59, 65, 80 n., 116
Wenamon, story of, 54, 62, 65
Wisdom literature, 139 f.
Wiseman, D. J., 122
Wood, J. T., 170
Woolley, Sir Leonard, 27
Wright, G. E., 77 n., 99 n.
Writing, 113 f., 141, 143

Yadin, Y., 50
Yahweh,
  acknowledged by Cyrus, 131
  anthropomorphic conception of, 18, 86
  Canaanite titles of, 8
  creator, 4 f.
  dwelling of, 86 ff.
  giver of fertility, 8
  and heavenly host, 5 f., 115
  'jealous' god, 17
  theory of Kenite origin, 41
  'living' god, 11
  lord of history, 4 f.
  no images of, 17 f., 82, 92
  patriarchal deity identified with, 32
  personification of aspects of, 134 f.
  presence of, 87 f.
  in proper names, 101, 103
  god of storm, 8, 40

Zabul, 7
Zedekiah, 121, 123 f.
Zephaniah, 117 f.
Zeus, 136
ziggurat, 26, 33, 83
Zion, 7, 73
Zoan, 29, 36 f.
Zoar, 30
Zobah, 69
Zoroastrianism, 156